ABOUT THE AUTHOR, AND THIS BOOK

I have been researching the 2012 ph
decade. Survive2012.com was launc. _____, and was the first
website dedicated to the topic. Since then I have maintained the
largest forum about 2012, as well as a wiki, web directory and social
network. Along with interacting with thousands of 2012ers, and
sharing ideas with prominent authors, I have amassed over 600
books related to the topic.

This book has evolved over the years. Initially my primary interest was
deciphering the meaning of 2012, working out what an ancient
culture may have predicted for us. This information is now freely
available at Survive2012.com, in the form of hundreds of blog posts,
and articles on topics ranging from pyramid bunkers to unicorns.

The finished book focuses on inspiring people to prepare for the
worst, just in case. I haven't filled it with fancy prose or superfluous
information. It is quick and to the point, but it is not short on relevant
information.

DISCLAIMER

The advice provided in this book is general in nature. I do not know your personal circumstances, and therefore the information within might not be suited to your needs. While some of the information has been garnered from personal experience, much of it has been researched.

The person responsible for your survival is yourself, and you need to use your own judgment. You should seek advice from as many books and people as you can, and think long and hard before making potentially life-changing decisions.

SURVIVE 2012

A Handbook For Doomsday Preppers

By Robert Bast

Contents

Appendices

This document has four main sections, and each is of equal importance. The third section covers the best general locations worldwide, as well as some specific locations for certain countries. Please don't skip the first two sections, for they relate to how to choose the best location for you. You need to consider what you think may occur in 2012 (or any other year), and you need to make a connection between your survival plans and your everyday life.

Oh, and congratulations on your purchase. You have now joined the top 0.01% of western civilization that is actively seeking to prepare for the worst, which means you and your family can and will be deliberate survivors.

Why 2012?

Everybody knows that the Long Count calendar of the ancient Maya ends on Dec 21, 2012. The puzzling aspect is what it might mean. Orthodox experts will tell you that it is just like our New Year's Eve, it will simply be followed by the first day of a new year, a year which for the Mayans was 5125 solar years long. They are correct.

What the "experts" choose to omit is what the Maya said about the previous three times the calendar ended. Each time the gods wiped out all humans via a natural disaster, and repopulated the planet with a new and improved human species. This is described in the ancient Mayan *Popul Vuh* text.

99.9% of Mayan books were burned by the conquering Spanish. Many monuments are undiscovered or still waiting to be deciphered. Of what we *have* read, there has been no indication of what the Mayans expected to happen in 2012. Pretty much all we have is this fragmentary inscription:

"The Thirteenth 'Bak'tun" will be finished (on) Four Ajaw, the Third of Uniiw (K'ank'in).
? will occur.
(It will be) the descent(??) of the Nine Support? God(s) to the ?."
(David Stuart's decipherment of Tortuguero Monument 6)

While I believe it means the gods will descend into their bunker, it really is open to interpretation. Unless more texts are discovered or announced soon, we must presume that they expected a natural disaster, just like the last three times the calendar ended.

There is a lot of misinformation online (and on cable TV) regarding a possible catastrophe in 2012. The possibilities can be divided into three groups:

New Age – these have no real scientific basis, but plenty of pseudo-science. Some mention *Earth Changes*, but typically the message is that we can avoid a disaster by thinking nice thoughts etc.

Bad Science – this covers every case where someone says a disaster will definitely occur in 2012, and a popular one is the return of Planet X / Nibiru (which certainly does not exist in a 2012 timeframe).

Real Science – genuine possibilities for TEOTWAWKI (the end of the world as we know it) and SHTF. This includes CMEs from the sun, supervolcanoes and an asteroid or comet crashing into our planet.

While any of the above could have been *prophesized* by the ancient Maya, so could the return of a giant purple bumblebee. Only real science could have really been used to make a genuine *prediction* for a 2012 disaster. In my opinion the only global cataclysms the Maya could have accurately predicted for 2012 are the return of an asteroid or comet, or a cyclical event from the Sun. Still, anything is possible and it would be best to prepare for all threats!

Section 1 - Possible Threats

Nobody knows for sure what will happen in 2012, so there's little point spending a lot of time pondering over exactly <u>what</u> will happen. Especially when the survival solution is almost always the same – *be somewhere else*.

Comet / Asteroid

There are two very different outcomes from an asteroid or comet colliding with our planet – a land strike or a sea strike. If it lands in the ocean, expect a mother of all tsunamis to destroy every coastline within its reach, and numerous miles inland. The tsunami could potentially be hundreds of meters in height. The good news is that once the seas have subsided, it's all over bar cleaning up and starting again.

If it strikes solid ground, then multiple scenarios become intertwined. An asteroid striking the ground will (depending on the approach angle) possibly disintegrate into thousands of pieces, each being relaunched into the atmosphere and then falling back down to Earth aflame. Whether it breaks up or not, the amount of dust and dirt flung into the air could cool the planet for many years.

If it does break up, then fires could be widespread and long-lasting. If this sounds Biblical, then perhaps it has happened before...

NB. In the unlikely event that news reports tell you the asteroid or comet is aimed right at your survival spot, then if you are fortunate to live on a continent – hit the road! It would be good to have in the back of your mind an alternate safe spot that you can get to by land, and a quiet route for getting there.

Tsunami

The good news is there's no such thing as a spontaneous tsunami. It has to be triggered by another event, by a geophysical disruption. Most likely candidates are earthquakes, asteroids/comets and landslides. Whether you get a warning or not is a factor of your proximity to the epicenter, and the availability of a local warning system.

Despite the great loss of life, the two major tsunamis of recent times are actually quite small compared to the biggest of all time, and what is physically possible. If you wish to prepare for the very worst, think of tsunamis hundreds of meters in height. Wikipedia lists the highest recorded mega-tsunamis of the last 500 years:

1792: Mount Unzen, Japan, 100 meters
1958: Lituya Bay, Alaska, USA, 524 meters (caused by a landslide)
1963: Vajont Dam, Italy, 250 meters (landslide above a dam)
1980: Spirit Lake, Washington, USA, 260 meters (Mt St Helens landslide)

An asteroid can crash anywhere, but at least we have some suspects for where the next tsunami causing landslide will be:

Cumbre Vieja volcano, Canary Islands. This volcano is dormant, but if and when it erupts again, the result could be a landslide, which in turn would create a tsunami one kilometer in height. By the time it reaches the East Coast of the USA and the Caribbean, it would still be 50 meters high and *millions* of people could die.

Mauna Loa volcano, Hawaii. Likewise, an eruption & landslide could cause a 1 kilometer high tsunami, and this actually happened 12,000 years ago. This time around, Honolulu would be wiped out just 30 minutes later.

Earthquake

Earthquakes happen all the time, and so far we have been unable to predict them. Many of the scenarios listed here could be accompanied by an earthquake – volcano, tsunami, asteroid/meteor, pole shift... So expecting an earthquake should be a key consideration when choosing a location and creating a safe spot.

Keep away from known fault lines. Don't be at the bottom of a slope. Don't be in cave, or house, or any structure that is not suitably reinforced. Don't have anything that can collapse above your bunker entrance. Within your bunker/basement/room make sure that things are secured.

A major earthquake in your area is good prompt to relocate. In less than a year since Christchurch's deadly earthquake, 20% of their citizens have moved away. They aren't survivalists; they're just using their gut instinct.

A very sobering map from NASA (below) shows all earthquake epicenters greater than Richter 3.5, 1963-1998. The places to avoid stand out a mile.

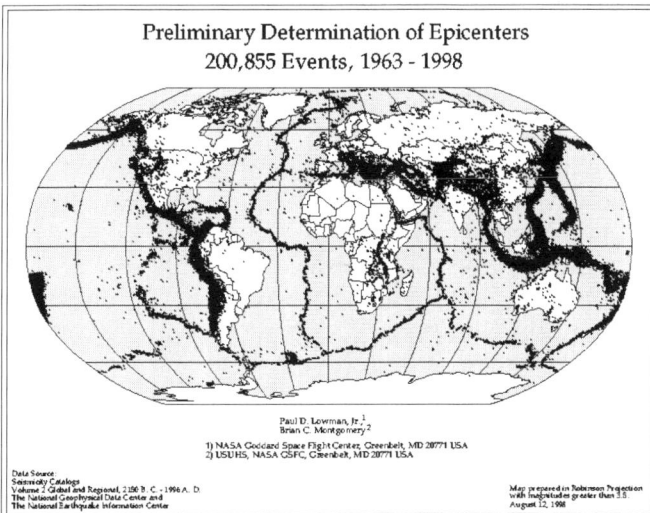

Preliminary Determination of Epicenters
200,855 Events, 1963 - 1998

Paul D. Lowman, Jr.[1]
Brian C. Montgomery[2]
1) NASA Goddard Space Flight Center, Greenbelt, MD 20771 USA
2) USUHS, NASA GSFC, Greenbelt, MD 20771 USA

Data Source:
Seismicity Catalogs
Volume 2 Global and Regional, 2150 B. C. - 1996 A. D.
The National Geophysical Data Center and
The National Earthquake Information Center

Map prepared in Robinson Projection
with magnitudes greater than 3.5.
August 12, 1998

Nuclear

In theory, a terrorist's dirty bomb could be used anywhere. And pretty much any city in the northern hemisphere could be hit by a nuclear missile. Nuclear power plants have a fixed location, so at least you can choose to avoid them.

FEMA describe two zones of safety in the case of a nuclear accident. Basically you want to be more than 10 miles away at the time of the accident, and you want to live more than 50 miles away afterwards. These are rough guides, and really depend on the speed and direction of the wind. I suggest a minimum of 100 miles between your safe spot and any potential nuclear disaster.

As we saw in 2011, a tsunami can lead to the meltdown of a nuclear power plant. Any event that damages the plant, or shuts off their electrical supply, can lead to meltdown. That list would include earthquakes, deliberate sabotage or terrorist attacks, loss of the power grid due to a CME, floods or tornadoes.

Volcano

A supervolcano would immediately wipe out surrounding populations, and ultimately place the human species in danger of extinction. If you are lucky, precursor tremors will alert you to the possible situation.

A smaller volcano will not endanger us to the same extent, but if it occurs in a key country of the global economy, the flow-on effect could be huge. As I write this, the volcanoes of Iceland seem poised to disrupt European air travel for extended periods of time. This will affect tourism, but also business travel, and more significantly, air freight. The butterfly effect of something as basic as mail delivery taking weeks instead of days has probably not been modelled, although I suspect it could cause a global recession.

(for more detailed information, see Appendix 4 at the end of the book)

Cosmic Radiation

This is a long-shot. While a mass influx of cosmic rays could explain mass extinctions, ancient climate change or even evolution, it's all just speculation. The problem is, we don't really know enough about where cosmic rays come from, and a lot of knowledge about outer space is based on assumptions.

Scientists assure us that there are no stars capable of going supernova in the near future, which are also near enough to harm us. Yet, just when they thought they had every type of star catalogued, they find something new. There *are* several nearby stars that are about ready to explode, and it wouldn't take much for the experts to be wrong about how safe we are.

The bottom line, the best place to be for safety from cosmic rays is under lead shielding, under a lot of concrete (a pyramid would do the trick), or underground.

Coronal Mass Ejection

It is conceivable that the ancient Mayans, or even a civilization that preceded them, could have tracked solar activities for millennia. And they could have picked up on a pattern that leads us to late 2012 / early 2013, a period in which solar activity for the current cycle is expected to peak.

Regardless of ancient predictions, there are two situations that can harm us globally, without warning – a Coronal Mass Ejection, or collision with an asteroid, comet or meteor storm. Supervolcanoes are a third possibility, although it is presumed that some form of pre-warning would be noticed.

A CME is a massive burst of energy from the Sun. It is often, but not always, associated with a solar flare. CMEs occur several times per day during the peak of the solar cycle, but because we are tiny compared to the Sun, we are rarely in their path.

When we are in the path of a CME, great harm can be inflicted upon us, especially now because of our reliance on electronics. If you stand outside during a CME that is directed towards Earth, you won't notice anything different. It won't be any warmer and you won't get sunburnt. Pretty much the only problem will be the harm done to electronics.

Depending on the intensity, the most likely result is no harm done. The next most likely is the damage to, and/or loss of a satellite. Or a few satellites. If it is any stronger it can take out transformers here on Earth, and beyond that an entire power grid could go down. The grids of Europe and the USA, due to their age, are especially susceptible.

A NASA report, *Severe Space Weather Events — Understanding Societal and Economic Impacts*, summed up how serious a risk CMEs are for the USA:

> "...more than 350 transformers at risk of permanent damage and 130 million people without power. The loss of electricity would ripple across the social infrastructure with "water distribution affected within several hours; perishable foods and medications lost in 12-24 hours; loss of heating/air conditioning, sewage disposal, phone service, fuel re-supply and so on."

Even if it is only satellites affected, serious chaos could result. The loss of GPS satellites would affect much more than just your Garmin or TomTom. Actually 90% of GPS receivers use the data for *timing* not location. If GPS signals are lost, these are some of the services that will be affected:

- Cell phone towers
- Air traffic control
- Emergency pagers
- ATM machines
- Electric grids
- Stock exchanges

...and navigation (obviously), but not just your car – think freight in a just-in-time environment, emergency services, shipping and train routing.

The first four of the above services were affected in San Diego for 2 hours in January 2007. The culprit was later discovered to be a naval exercise nearby, where they blocked radio signals.

(for more detailed information, see Appendix 1 at the end of the book)

A CME Scenario

Imagine this. Your electricity is switched off, without warning. You check with your neighbors, and it looks like your whole street has been affected. Oh well, it's Saturday night, so you get out some flashlights and play charades with your family. At bedtime you go to fetch a glass of water and realize that water is off as well. *Somebody will fix these things* you think as you drift off to sleep.

The next morning there's still no electricity or water. And you've just realized that your landline and cell phone aren't working either. You are discussing it with your neighbor when you notice somebody reversing out of their driveway, the station wagon packed to the brim, as well as the roof rack. Turns out they heard a radio news report that said it could take weeks for services to be up and running again, so they are heading to a friend's farm.

With no farm to go to, you decide you better stock up on some supplies, but it is too late. Everywhere is closed. Supermarkets, gas stations, shopping malls, restaurants. ATMs aren't working. Many premises are guarded by their owners, brandishing rifles. Some businesses, especially supermarkets, have already been ransacked.

No food, no water, no money. No heating or cooling. No way of calling for help. And when the government says weeks, the reality is that it could be almost a year before everything is back to normal.

And then you hear a rumor that a nearby nuclear facility is in meltdown...

Magnetic Pole Shift

Science has not yet determined the mechanism of a magnetic pole shift, but by studying the magnetism of ancient rocks they can tell that shifts have occurred many times in the past. The magnetic north pole is rapidly moving across Canada. The strength of our planet's magnetic field is rapidly diminishing. While we do not know if these factors are relevant or not, it makes sense to prepare for the worst.

A flip of the magnetic poles would primarily affect navigation – anything that uses a compass, and those birds and animals that are tuned in biologically. Basically, pigeons get lost and planes crash.

If the flip coincides with a lack of magnetic field, then we could suffer terribly for the duration of the flip. The electromagnetic field keeps our planet safe from harmful radiation from our Sun and from space. Without that shield, crops, animals and people who are not undercover will burn, or suffer from mutations.

According to orthodox science, a pole shift would take hundreds or thousands of years. The fatal flaw is that, if historical shifts had happened overnight, science would not be able to detect such a rapid change. To do so would require the ability to tell that one rock is one day older, after thousands or millions of years, than another. The notion that it will take a thousand years is a derivative of the resolution of the data available to them.

It could happen while you are sleeping. It is presumed that sudden and unusual weather would be an indicator – if a news service hadn't already told you.

Crustal Pole Shift

This concept is not accepted by orthodox science, although it has had some distinguished fans, including Albert Einstein. While there is evidence for displacements in relatively recent geological times, the sticking point is a lack of internal mechanism.

With a displacement, the Earth's outer crust moves rapidly (as opposed to the extremely slow movement due to plate tectonics) and slips relative to the core. The result is that land masses end up being located at a different latitude/longitude than before the shift. A famous piece of evidence for such a shift is the graveyard of mammoths in Siberia. The mammoths were snap frozen. One specimen was chewing on a plant when he died - a plant that does not live in arctic zones. The supposition is that the mammoths were living in a more temperate region, and a sudden pole shift transported them to the Arctic.

According to Charles Hapgood, the shifts were roughly 30-40 degrees in nature, and the last one occurred approximately 12,000 years ago.

A crustal displacement is featured in the recent blockbuster movie *2012*.

Civil Unrest

This is vastly under-appreciated, and past instances – in Western societies – are conveniently forgotten. In Europe, the USA and Australia riots have been shorter-lived and less impactful than in other lands, such as in the Middle East in 2011. That comes down to motivation. While both are generally triggered by a small (but not trivial) incident such as self-immolation or a death in custody, those in the west have not generally sought a change in power. If a government is seen to be inept during a catastrophe, causing people to suffer, they can and will fight back in any society.

Unless you are someone wanting to cause unrest, the safest place for you and your family will be somewhere else.

Military Invasion

Large, stable democracies (and their allies) are unlikely to suffer a military invasion - in normal times. However, in conjunction with some of the other events listed, it is a possibility. For example, a volcano could devastate a country, leaving it vulnerable to an attack from a neighbor.

Terrorism

We are fortunate that terrorists tend to prefer explosions, and have mostly ignored attacking infrastructure. If someone really wanted to, and had the right skills, they could, conceivably:

- Hack into a nuclear power plant and cause meltdown
- Hack into the power grid and cause it to fail
- Contaminate water supplies
- Interrupt GPS reception
- Shut down ATMs
- Cause stock market chaos

Remember, don't just think of these as isolated possibilities. Several facilities could be attacked at once, or they could choose to strike during a natural disaster.

Global Warming / Climate Change

It is my considered opinion that Anthropogenic (man-made) Global Warming is negligible and not worth worrying about. Temperatures were rising until the end of last century, but the links between temperature changes and human activity are poor. I wouldn't be surprised if we are heading towards a cold spell, especially if the next solar peak (in 2012/2013) is as weak as some predict.

I believe climate change is very real and probably driven by our Sun. The activities of our Sun are notoriously difficult to predict, and that gives us an additional reason to be prepared. If temperatures were to quickly rise or drop by a few degrees, then the effects on crops will be considerable. This would most likely trigger food-shortages, which could then trigger civil unrest. You might want to be in your safe spot, with your supplies, until things calm down.

If temperatures start to rise again, our weather will become less stable. This is where the butterfly effect comes in to play. Most people in the USA's east coast have noticed the increased number of hurricanes each year. That's only the beginning. Floods are also increasing. And there is concern that next up could be a destabilization of the North Atlantic Current...

Before the *2012* movie, Roland Emmerich made *The Day After Tomorrow*, a disaster flick which showed the effects of a rapid-onset ice age. Most people are unaware that the film is based on a non-fiction book, *The Coming Global Superstorm*, in which global warming causes enough of the ice caps to melt that the salinity in the Atlantic lessens, leading to changes in the Gulf Stream and North Atlantic Current. The end result is an instant ice age.

Mini Ice Age

In *The Day After Tomorrow* we are asked to believe that our planet's climate is capable of rapid change, and according to scientists from the University of Saskatchewan it is possible.

> Around 12,800 years ago the northern hemisphere was hit by the Younger Dryas mini ice age or "Big Freeze...and lasted around 1300 years.
>
> Until now, it was thought that the mini ice age took a decade or so to take hold, on the evidence provided by Greenland ice cores.

...The group studied a mud core from an ancient lake, Lough Monreagh, in western Ireland. Using a scalpel they sliced off layers 0.5 to 1 millimeter thick, each representing up to three months of time. No other measurements from the period have approached this level of detail.

...They show that at the start of the Big Freeze, **temperatures plummeted** and lake productivity stopped **within months**, or a year at most. "It would be like taking Ireland today and moving it up to Svalbard" in the Arctic, says Patterson.

The drop in temperatures averaged 5 degrees globally, but as much as 15 degrees in Greenland. The date of the mini ice age, and the rapid onset, suggest a global cataclysm caused by a pole shift or asteroid/comet. Numerous books have been recently hypothesizing either scenario, and this recent evidence makes their ideas even more compelling.

Not only would normal activities and crops be under pressure, a universal lack of preparation would compound the problems. For example, massive increases in energy use to keep people warm, as well as shortages of heating equipment. Sea passages would close, planes would be grounded, and trains wouldn't run. Pipes will burst. And on top of it all, people will be scared and confused, untrusting of scientists. Many will be seeking to move south, too many at once.

Water Shortage

There are two ways that water might become an issue. The first is that water is available, but becomes very expensive due to more people wanting to access dwindling supplies. The second is where supplies become contaminated – something terrorists can easily achieve - or it could be the result of a natural event, like volcanic ash in water reservoirs.

To cover all eventualities, it would be prudent to maintain a large supply of stored water, as well as making sure your safe spot has its own water supplies. Typically this would be via a bore or well (easy to keep ash out), a lake or river, or by collecting rainwater.

Food Shortage

This could be a result of many of the scenarios listed here, or it can happen on its own, via over-population or crop disease, or war. The simple answer is to have lots of food supplies in storage, and to purchase them prior to the general public deciding to do the same. You will also need to consider that you will own a valuable commodity in what could be a fragile and dangerous community. Therefore it is critical that you do not tell anyone about the extent of your supplies, ever. It is the sort of thing that people will recall after a catastrophe, that so-and-so has 10 giant bags of rice. Friends will pressure you to share (share by all means, but for it to be on your terms means keeping quiet about it beforehand), and others may be tempted to steal from you – desperate measures for desperate times.

It is also critical that you don't keep all your supplies in one place, and they are well hidden. Under a blanket in your garage is not good, in the attic is better, and buried somewhere is really good.

Over-Population

This certainly won't happen overnight. That doesn't mean we should be complacent. It is feasible that the strains of over-population could cause an event somewhere which then initiates a domino effect. More likely is that the effects are slow, and generally speaking, those who chose the path of self-sufficiency earlier would do better.

Plan on Being Wrong

It saddens me to see so many people who are certain X will occur in 2012, and have based their survival plans around their own dead-set ideas. I've been telling people until I am blue in the face – nobody knows what will happen in 2012! It is quite likely that the event is something nobody thought of.

Don't become too obsessed with your own ideas, or those of someone else because they seemed genuine in a YouTube video, or their book has an authoritative tone. 2012 could be your undoing – so swallow your pride and prepare for all the things you doubt will happen.

Section 2 - You and Your Safe Spot

In Section 3 I will describe the safest places to be, worldwide. My research has obviously not taken into account your own personal circumstances. Here are some ideas to help you make a considered decision.

When?

Aside from the ancient Mayan Long Count calendar that ends on Dec 21, 2012 – your need for a safe spot could arrive at any time. More than likely it will be short notice rather than long. Do not underestimate your fellow citizens. When news gets out that something is going wrong in the world, survival instincts will kick in – supermarket shelves will be emptied, highways will be clogged, and some people will choose violence as a means to an end.

Regarding Dec 21, 2012 – this is the winter solstice in the Northern hemisphere (summer solstice in the Southern hemisphere). The odds of the calendar ending on a solstice or equinox is roughly 1 in 91. It is quite likely (in my opinion) that the winter solstice, the darkest day of the year, was chosen for psychological impact, rather than the precise event date. If this is the case, then the 2012 event could occur 6 months either side of Dec 2012.

My recommendation is that you spend a week or two either side of Dec 21, 2012 at your bunker location, and six months either side of that date in a state of high alert, monitoring everything monitor-able. Outside of that timeframe, relax. Have plans in place, but don't be too focused on the potential doomsday – otherwise you could end up spending the rest of your life in fear of something that never happens, and that would be a waste!

How Much Preparation?

It's not just money; it's time and potential embarrassment. For many of us, spending every spare moment building a bunker will cause your friends to reconsider their relationship with you. It is important that you determine how much your survivalist efforts are worth to you in terms of social sacrifice. And how things might pan out post-2012.

The key factors are shelter, food and water. Have these in place and everything else can be worked out. Keep in mind that post-2012 you may have lots of time on your hands...

Costs

There are a lot of 2012 "experts" out there, but as far as I know I am the only one who has dared to declare the odds of a bad event occurring in 2012. I have plucked 10% out of my hat. It's my best guess, but only a guess, and based on nothing tangible. You need to consider the likelihood of you actually needing a safe spot, in 2012, or beyond. Dig deep and come up with your own odds, your own prediction. And then base your degree of survival preparations on that judgment.

It's a cruel fact of life that those most in tune with the risks of 2012 and beyond are the least capable of preparing – financially. People with high incomes tend to be too busy to notice, or feel too immune.

Keep in mind that if you borrow to buy your survival property, in 2012 terms your only costs will be a couple of year's worth of mortgage repayments. If nothing happens in 2012, you can sell. If something does happen, there might not be any banks that survive... Of course there are additional costs associated with buying and selling, as well as any building work you may undertake.

The most expensive option is to build a bunker. Tom Cruise reportedly spent $10 million on his. I'm planning on spending roughly $150,000. There's no reason why a functional, underground bunker cannot be built for $20,000 or so. A key question is how long you will have to be inside your bunker. Most scenarios I am aware of will not require more than three days underground, however some scenarios could see you down there for years. Examples include radioactive contamination, a long-term cosmic ray bombardment, civil unrest and very extreme hot or cold weather.

In a three-day bunker you can survive on bottled water, compost toilets and battery power, with the main technical consideration being ventilation. It should not cost much more to build than a swimming pool.

A bunker that protects people for years becomes expensive and complicated. Ventilation, waste disposal, water, power... On top of that, considerations of how your group will cope mentally during long-term confinement.

I suggest that if you build a bunker you prepare for either a short-term scenario (less than a week) or a long-term scenario (more than two years).

A bunker might not be necessary. Many homes (especially in the USA and Europe) already have basements. Basements are great for surviving many situations. About the only negative is the house above could collapse and block your exit.

And there are possibilities where simply being away from it all will suffice, so long as you can be self-sufficient. For example, nuclear war in the Northern Hemisphere is not predicted to directly affect those in Australia, southern Africa or South America. But the associated financial meltdown, and lack of crops, will make having your own rural plot appealing.

If you cannot purchase land in a safe spot, consider alternatives. Safe spots tend to be rural, and include government land. Investigate your rights to camp there – you might even be able to take out a seasonal pass.

Befriend a property owner, and joke about the potential for you to crash with them if something bad goes down.

Locate properties that are not being used. In an extreme situation you may be able to claim them as your own. It could be anything from an abandoned pig-sty to a mine shaft.

If your safe spot is in a sparsely populated area, and the locals are generous and friendly, perhaps all you need to do is turn up. If you are the only "refugee", it's quite likely that you will be taken in.

You could even hitchhike to your safe spot, given enough advance warning... totally free survival is a possibility

Buy a Berth

There are a few bunker communities being built where the only requirements are that you pay the fee (from $50,000 to $500,000) and promise to be good. While some might get off the ground, most won't, so make sure any money you deposit is kept in trust by a third-party.

If the bunker does become reality, and 2012 does experience a terrible event, and you do manage to get to the mega-bunker, and it is in a good spot, and everyone in it survives... keep in mind that there has probably been little thought put into what happens next.

The person/people in charge of the bunker scheme might not be good at leading, which means you could end up being lead by anyone. Your bunker mates will be those without the resources to have built their own safe spot, and without the ability to get things done on their own. They will probably be easily led, and whatever the group decides, you will need to go along with.

The most likely scenario I can imagine is that you will end up being led by someone who is ex-military or ex-police. They will not be very democratic. There will be plenty of potential for things to go terribly wrong. And if outside is unsafe (war, radiation, extreme weather), you will be stuck with them.

Proximity

There is nothing more important than the ability to get to your safe spot. If you are unable to get there in time, or even get there at all, then your preparations would be wasted. There are three timeframes that seem to fit an event that needs surviving; instant, a few days, and ongoing decline. An example of instant is a tsunami warning. A few days could be an approaching asteroid. And ongoing could be global warming.

You need to think deeply about every scenario you believe is possible, and work out how easy/hard it will be to get to your spot, given that the whole world could be in a state of panic, and given that the world may have begun to fall apart. Highways could be clogged. Bridges may have collapsed. Is there an alternate route that is free of hindrances?

Ultimately, accessibility being equal, the closer your spot is to your everyday life, the better. Ideally you will already be at your spot when the event happens, but that may require an extremist attitude unsuited to long-term preparedness. Yet for December 2012, it could be easily achieved by just taking your annual vacation.

Other Uses

When the PlayStation 2 first came out, every game-playing husband knew that it was a video game console that happened to play DVDs. What they told their wives was that it was a state-of-the-art DVD player that happens to also have games.

And so it can be for many safe spot scenarios. For me personally, my wife misses the holiday home of her childhood, the comfort of vacationing in the same place year after year. And I feel that I benefited from growing up in the countryside. This means that for my family, who aren't particularly interested in 2012, the farm is a place for weekends away, for communing with nature. However, it is *my* farm, and I'm allowed to build a bunker to play in.

Family + Friends

It is most likely that few of your friends or relatives will be interested in your madcap ideas about the "end of the world". But if and when that day comes, they are bound to recall that you have made preparations, and they will want in.

It is a balancing act. While you certainly do not want your neighborhood to know you have a bunker or supplies, it would be beneficial to have people you know and trust along for the ride. Make sure that when you share your plans with others, that you wouldn't mind spending weeks or years in a bunker with them, along with the acquaintances whom your story gets passed on to.

Ultimately it might not matter who knows, if only your favorite people know where your spot is, and have visited it. While they might tell random strangers about your preparations, they are unlikely to hand out an address. Therefore the key people to not share your plans with are your neighbors (unless they are friends). Neighbors already know your address...

Escaping

Beat the pack, be ahead of the hordes, and get out first. Not only will this mindset help you avoid traffic jams, it might get you to your spot before whatever-it-is happens. This means keeping your ear to the ground – don't be someone that hears about the SHTF on the 6pm news. Get a smart phone, subscribe to news feeds and alerts (volcanoes, earthquakes, tsunamis...), and check the news regularly. Don't wait for 100% verification that something bad is happening; you can always return home if it was a false alarm. Here are some key factors to also consider:

- Avoid vulnerable roads. Be wary of tunnels, bridges with no alternate route, potential landslides, potential flooding.
- Practice getting to your spot using back roads, work out multiple ways of getting there.
- Have your car and bags already packed.
- Have your supplies already purchased.
- Make sure you always have a full tank of gas.

Sometimes, no matter how prepared you are, fate will spoil your plans. Along your chosen escape routes, look for many places that will be good spots if you can't get out of the city. Most preferable are underground structures that are easy to get out of after an earthquake. This could be shopping mall car parks, homes with basements, train stations and tunnels. Even a culvert could be substantially better than sitting in your car.

Say your car won't start. Aside from the possibility of acquiring another vehicle, know all the homes and buildings in your neighbourhood that have better survivability than your own home. Commercial properties are likely to be abandoned, and if you turn up to someone's home with survival gear, they could welcome you with open arms.

If you will be evacuating on your own, consider a motorcycle, preferably of the dual-sport type. You won't be able to carry much, but your odds of reaching your safe spot are improved immensely. Fuel is still probably going to be a problem, but if your only hope of escape is via blocked freeways, a motorcycle could be the ticket.

Letting Strangers In

Charitable readers who build bunkers might consider sharing their space with people they don't know so well. It might be a friend of a friend, or even a complete stranger who you met online. It is a lovely thought, yet the risks are numerous. Unless you know someone really well, my advice is that you do not plan on surviving alongside them.

At every level of society, from the government and military, to school committees and street sweepers, there will always be some who wish to dictate how things are done, and those who will happily follow, and many in-between. It is important that you know your survival companions well enough to have an idea of how they will react in group situations, and when things go wrong.

You also may be unaware of a person's mental health, addictions, sexual needs/desires, violent tendencies, greed, delusions and so on. If you do take on strangers, make sure your leadership is strong, and that you have facilities for locking up those who do not play ball.

Panic

In a SHTF-2012 scenario, it is critical that panic does not affect your odds of survival. Have you ever packed for an overseas trip a few hours before the plane departs? And in the taxi you are wondering if you locked the doors, if you packed your passport? A SHTF scenario is a one-off, and you are not naturally pre-programmed to cope, not like a holiday. If you have not made meticulous plans and had a few dry-runs, it is almost guaranteed that 10 minutes after heading off to your safe spot you will realize you have forgotten something critical, and will have the dilemma of returning to collect it, or carrying on without it. This is why you should have a "go bag" or even a ready-packed "go vehicle".

Go Bag / Go Vehicle

A "go bag" contains all the little things that go a long way in an emergency. Typical inclusions are a torch, matches, bottle of water, radio, energy bars, identification and so on. The sorts of things that could make a night out in the wild more comfortable.

A "go vehicle" is more advanced, and substantially more useful – entirely due to the increased capacity and mobility. It is also a luxury that you may not be able to afford... but if you can manage it, make sure you have one.

The nature of a "go vehicle" means that it is not routinely used for anything else, aside from transporting the driver and a passenger – because the rest of the interior will be full. If it is just for yourself, your vehicle can contain enough food, water and fuel for a long journey. And of course a car can protect you from the elements.

Stashes

If you are storing food etc, be inventive about where you put it. Although the pantry or garage of your safe spot would be the traditional place to store supplies, it is also the easiest place for thieves to find them. Consider burying portions of your supplies, and maintaining a minimum in the open. In the greater scheme of things, a bit of digging will be a small price to pay for such security.

Example Go Bag

You won't be able to fit all of these in a handy bag, so choose the items that you believe will be of the most use to you:

Torch / Flashlight. Don't go cheap! Maglites are rightly famous. Generally speaking, most small stainless steel torches that take AA or AAA batteries will be alright. Thinking beyond a 3-day crisis, consider a solar powered and/or hand-cranked flashlight. Word of warning – the crank handle on cheap products will often not last very long, because the act of cranking places a lot of pressure on the handle. Don't go cheap!
Radio. Not knowing what is going on can be terrifying, so make sure you have a reliable radio. One that takes batteries as well as being solar or hand-crankable is ideal. Try and get one that receives shortwave – my Summit Freeplay does.
Water. You can't get dehydrated water, so how much you think you will need equals the space/weight it will take. Plastic bottles are lighter, and err on the side of more water. A person needs two liters / half a gallon per day, minimum. Three two-liter bottles will take up half the space in a small backpack - you just have to accept it.
Food. Snack bars have a high ratio of energy to weight and size. Chocolate and nuts are good as well. Carbohydrates are too bulky. Tip: taste and personal preference will not matter in a SHTF scenario – you will be willing to eat anything.
Protective clothing. Gloves might prove to be handy. A lightweight poncho can keep you dry. A fresh pair of socks or underwear could save blisters and chaffing.
iPad / Kindle. Or a smart phone, or an iPod Touch. Or a netbook. The key criteria are being able to go online (over cell networks is a bonus), and storing survivalism ebooks – there are a lot out there that you can grab for free... Knowledge is king.

ID. Copies of your various forms of ID, credit cards, proof of citizenship or residency, driver's license. Where you keep your original is up to you. All but one of my originals are at my safe spot. My driver's license is on me.

Printed maps. The best scale available for where you figure you will end up. Some maps are accurate they show properties and buildings. Presume all electronics will fail and have some old school maps with you.

Something valuable. Imagine getting mugged. The mugger wants a reward for their crime. If you can give them something they perceive to be valuable, they might depart happy, not harming you. Try offering something shiny if your practical items don't impress.

Knives. Difficult in that carrying a knife is illegal in many lands. If you think it will be OK, get yourself a short machete.

Cash. In the transition between SHTF and everyone adjusting, cash will have some value. A few hundred dollars could be useful, and if 2012 never happens it will be a nice little nest egg.

Hat and sunglasses. Depending on where you live, these can make marching through an afternoon more pleasant.

Entertainment. This is more for a long-term scenario, but you won't really know the scenario length when you initially flee... pack of cards, knucklebones, miniature Bible, whatever you like, as long as it can improve your mood

First Aid Kit. Most reputable ready-made kits will do. At a minimum it will contain bandages, tape, dressings, antibacterial ointment, alcohol and safety pins. Beyond that, it depends on how much space you are willing to sacrifice. Unless you are trained, have a manual. Also make sure you have any medications you depend on.

Photos of Loved Ones. Light and easy to carry, powerful motivator.

Space Blanket. Takes up almost no space and can keep you warm or cool out in the open.

Duct Tape. Along with a tarp and paracord, it's a classic multi-use item.

Paracord. Either in wristband or belt form, or have a bundle in your bag. As it comes it is great for tying and securing, but if you undo it, inside are thin enough threads to use for sewing or fishing.

Water purification. Whichever method you choose, have it with you, and have more than you think you could possibly need. That way you could end up saving the lives of others.

Zip-lock Freezer Bags. Keeps food fresh, and can hold water or other liquids. Also good for keeping things dry.

Fire Lighters. Plural. Have matches, have cigarette lighters, and have some flint and steel tools.

Batteries. Spares for whatever devices you are taking with you, and in case you bump into someone who needs them.

Dental Floss. Tough and compact, great for tying.

Sunscreen.

Mirror and Whistle. Good for being found in the wilderness. Not just by authorities, but if you are separated from others in your party.

Spare spectacles (if you wear them). If they are prescription sunglasses, they become dual-purpose.

Tin opener. If you have found one that is reliable and durable, buy a dozen. Carry two with you, some in the car, and some at your safe spot.

Sanitary napkins. Excellent for stopping bleeding.

Comfortable shoes. Have these alongside your go bag, ready to change in to.

Pocket Binoculars. Wondering if those people up ahead are friendly? Take a closer look. Small binoculars can still do the job.

Make sure the go bag itself is easy and comfortable to carry. The very nature of SHTF is that you will not know where and how far you might need to carry it. If your workplace is away from your home, either take your bag with you each day, or have a duplicate bag at work.

Additional Items for Your Car

As well as the following, have the items above, just more of each, because you can. Think carefully about how much you fill your vehicle. Consider that you might want to access something fast. Consider that you might need extra space to transport something or someone.

Tarpaulin. One of those items that you'll always find a use for. Things can go on it, under it or be wrapped up in it.

Tent. If you don't make it to your safe spot, you might have to camp. A tent will be a whole lot nicer than sleeping in your car.

Food and Water. Make sure the water containers aren't too heavy; mine are 10 liters (2.5 gallons). For your car, the food should be tinned.

Blankets.

Sleeping Bags.

Walkie Talkies. Cheap and legal, perfect for short-range communications while on the move, or at your safe spot.

Night Vision Goggles.

Garbage Bags. A small roll has a lot of bags.

Wet Wipes. For cleaning things when water is scarce.

Gasoline / Diesel. Make sure you understand how to store it, and the need to rotate it.

Cooking Pot and Lid. Aside from the obvious, a good cast iron pot can be used for storage, and if you fill it with items it won't take up much space.

Portable toilet. Can also have items stored within. Take toilet paper as well!

Tools (in a tool box).

Rope. Make sure it is strong enough to tow another vehicle.

Survival Guides. In print form, but try to have them on a screen device as well.

First Aid Kit. The bigger, the better. And make sure it has a manual. Don't cut corners on this item.

You don't have to store everything in your car. It will only take one minute to transfer some storage containers from your garage. The very best - but pricey - solution is to have a second car that is primarily for escape. It sits in your garage, fully laden, and full of fuel, waiting. Make sure you take it for a drive every now and then...

If you have a dedicated go car, there are two important considerations. An EMP attack could render a modern car useless. And in a long-term scenario, if you have a popular model there will be spare parts available to buy, barter or scavenge. My vehicle of choice is a Toyota Hilux Dual Cab with an enclosed rear that you cannot see into.

On Your Person

There may be times when you don't have your go bag handy (for example a dinner date), times when disaster could strike. More extreme than a go bag is carrying survival items on your person. I wouldn't start wearing a vest with 20 pockets everywhere I went, but consider these:

Motorola Defy+ cell phone – the most sturdy, water-resistant smart phone available and it is quite cheap. Store survival eBooks on it. And of course it is very useful if phone services and GPS satellites aren't down. Most smart phones have a torch / flashlight app available.

Casio Pathfinder watch – they are "shockproof", and mine is solar-powered, with a compass and altimeter and thermometer.

Survival Straps (available from survivalstraps.com) – 15 feet of paracord wound into an attractive wristband, or up to 200 feet in a belt.

Leatherman Squirt (or similar) – a multi-tool that goes on your key ring. Scissors, knife, pliers, wire cutter, screwdrivers and a bottle opener. Two inches long and weighs just two ounces. Use your own judgment as to whether it constitutes carrying a knife in your jurisdiction.

Gold Necklace. Make sure it is real gold! Cut off links when you need them for trading purposes.

I have the first four items on me whenever I'm not at home. Not only can they be incredibly useful in a survival situation, but they are excellent conversation pieces! People will ask you why you carry a multi-tool with you, or what that *different-looking* wristband is all about.

Identification. This might be very important post-event, so consider having key pieces of ID in each location, even if they are only photo copies. Make sure that you carry a piece of ID on your person at all times, such as a driver's license.

Cache

Consider a location that is part of the way to your desired safe spot, and use it to store supplies. Now this could be a secluded parcel of land, a building of some sort, or ideally a run-down but functional home with some acres in a location where properties are cheap. This serves a dual-purpose - if you cannot make it your safe spot, for whatever reason, you can retreat to your cache. Alternatively lease a drive-up unit at a self-storage facility. One large enough to contain a vehicle and supplies can be had for as little as $100 per month. You might even be able to write it off as a business expense.

Meeting Places

If phones aren't working, how will you rendezvous with family and friends? Make sure you have predetermined places to meet. Don't just say "we'll meet at home". Home might not be a safe place to be. Meet at A, but if A is not an option, meet at B, and so on. For my family, B is an underground car park, C is an abandoned factory along our safe place journey, and D is our safe place.

Camping and Vacations

If thinking about all of the above ideas has your head in a spin, and you know deep down that being fully prepared is something you will only dream about, then there is an easier option.

The key to initial survival is being somewhere relatively safe. Regardless of any other forms of preparation, being in a safe location when the SHTF will be better than being somewhere un-safe.

Most people take an annual vacation. For your 2012 vacation (ideally in December, but the months either side of Dec 21 2012 could also be disaster-prone) why not head somewhere safe? If you always have a beach vacation, how about just once in your life you spend some time in the hills?

Not everyone can afford a vacation, especially not an international one, but you don't *have* to stay in a hotel. Perhaps you have relatives you can go visit. For the very cheapest holiday, consider camping. Some of the safe spots I list are well-suited to camping.

One Last Thing – Do it!

The 2012 event (if it happens) won't be what kills you, your family and your friends. The ultimate cause, given that by reading this you are already concerned and aware of the possibilities, will be your own lack of action. Apathy is a modern problem. In prosperous countries it is all too easy to "get by" without putting much thought into things, without planning and following through with those plans. **Do you want apathy to be your final label?**

Section 3 - Global Safe Spots

This section of the book is, to my knowledge, quite unique. Patrick Geryl has indicated a few places he considers to be safe (South Africa and Sierra Nevada) and Lawrence E. Joseph has nominated a town in the USA. Stan Deyo moved to Australia to be safe, but he and his wife are back in the USA now. There are some "flood maps" floating about, but they pretty much just advise you to be away from the coast.

There's also quite an extensive list of safe spots that was prepared by the ZetaTalk folk, but it is solely concerned with a pole shift due to the passing of Planet X that an alien being told them about. I do not endorse it.
http://www.zetatalk.com/safelocs.pdf

Here are the factors I took into consideration:

IMPORTANT CRITERIA

No Nukes (no nuclear power plants or missiles or dumps or targets) within 100 miles

No Volcanoes or Calderas (active or dormant) within 200 miles

No Major Earthquakes - none in modern history, not on a fault line

No War Nearby - use own judgment

Not near a sand desert - sand storms can be nasty, but not always

Nothing above – landslide, dam, snow that can melt, glacier, lake

Not Near a Large Population >250,000 people - too many survivors after what you have

Clear Land Available - forests and woods can catch fire, so build on clear land

600 Meters above Sea-Level (or 2/5 of a mile) <u>and/or</u> 400 Kilometers Inland (or 250 miles)

Fertile Soil

Drinkable Water

Accessible (road/rail/airport)

Near a Town/City >20,000 people (supplies now, scavenge later perhaps)

Close to your current home - that way you might actually do it, rather than just plan and dream

DESIRABLE

Be on a continent - so that if your location turns out to be no good (especially climate-wise), you are able to travel by foot to somewhere better.

Be more than 54 degrees from the pole – pretty much the *only* information on the scope of crustal displacements comes from Charles Hapgood, and his research suggests that 3 previous crustal pole shifts each involved approximately 30 degrees of movement. This means that anywhere north or south of the 36 degree latitude line has a 50/50 chance of ending up being within the Arctic Circle, in the event of crustal displacement. Unless the shift is to the east or west! It is all very inexact, based on a theory with no known mechanism, but if you want a rule of thumb – if it already snows at your survival spot, a cooler planet could render it uninhabitable.

Modern, Western Civilization - it's just easier if that is what you are used to, and, big generalization, probably safer for you before and after. Obviously your own culture/country should be your first choice if you like it.

Hippies and Amish – if the local folk are keen on self-sufficiency, that could be a big plus, post-SHTF.

Nice Weather! – it is hard to build a bunker if you are snowed under, in a monsoon, or in scorching heat.

Not on a "flee path" – if everyone in a major city gets in their car and tries to escape, don't be at the first safe spot they come across. Or the second...

Please don't skip to your country or state! There are tips throughout, many of which will apply to your particular circumstances.

NOTE – have an atlas or Google Maps handy and look up places that interest you. Perhaps see how they relate to where you live. This is much better for you than if I provide little maps here with little flags on them...

Australia

I live in Australia, so when I tell you it is the safest place to be, you might think I'm a little bit biased. Well, I wasn't born in Australia, but "over the ditch" in New Zealand. I have spent considerable amounts of time in the USA and Europe, and my wife is English. My career is web-based and we could live anywhere in the world. Despite the appeal of some tax havens, we choose to live in Australia due to the culture, the prosperity, but above all we like the safety.

Australia has no nuclear power plants, and its exposure to earthquakes and volcanoes is minimal. It has a modern, western culture, and it is unlikely to have many neighbors turn up as it is surrounded by ocean. Population density is quite low, and it has substantially more arable land per person than any other country. Americans and Brits have no trouble fitting in.

New England Tablelands, NSW

In and around the major towns (Glen Innes, Armidale & Guyra) are excellent spots for 2012 and non-2012 possibilities. The region is named after England because it has a similar climate, with distinct seasons, plenty of rain and cold winters. It has a lot more water than most places in non-tropical Australia, and will easily withstand any global warming. The towns are roughly 1000m above sea level, and 150km from the coast. Populations are between 1800 and 20,000 people, yet it is easy to drive to Brisbane in an afternoon. There is at least one intentional community in the area, where you can join with as little as $20,000. If you are looking to purchase land, 4-5 acres close to a town are available for $150K, or for the same price you can buy 100 acres, only 30 minutes drive away.

Several wind farms are proposed for the area.

Glen Innes, NSW, Australia is my <u>#1 safe spot,</u> worldwide.

Glen Innes is the highest large town in Australia, with 6000 people at 1000 meters above sea level. The climate is mild, and there is plenty of rain. Winters are a bit on the cold side, but snow is infrequent.

There's plenty of accommodation, including caravan parks and farm stays. Bullock Mountain Homestead has the well-regarded pub crawls on horseback where you literally ride horses to a pub and spend the night there. Three Waters High has camping and cabins, with the option of fossicking for sapphires. They also accept WWOOFers (willing workers on organic farms), which means you get to stay for free in exchange for doing some work.

Glen Innes is home to the Australian Standing Stones, inspired by the Ring of Brodgar in Scotland's Orkneys. It was erected to honor the Celtic people who first settled in the area. Each summer solstice, Dec 21, there is a celebration at the stones.

Although Glen Innes is a farming community, alternative lifestyles are well represented, with several intention communities nearby. The best known of these is Wytaliba which has roughly 100 adults and children resident – and it even has its own government-funded school.

At the time of writing, 3 acres near the township was selling for $95,000. And just 10 kilometers north of Glen Innes is a cottage with 100 acres for just $129,000.

Central Tablelands, NSW

This locality is quite similar to the New England Tablelands, being east of the dividing range, at a similar elevation. Orange is 860m above sea level, and has a population of 32,000. It is handy to Sydney (260 kms) and has a temperate climate. Lots of fruit are grown here (strangely not including oranges – it isn't warm enough) and there are wineries. Nearby Blayney has 5 acre properties for $150K, and Cudal has 20 acres for a similar price.

Blayney has a 15 turbine wind farm, one of the largest in NSW.

Beechworth, Victoria

This town sits at an elevation of 560m, with a small population of just 3500. It has an excellent survival climate of not too hot and not too cold – the mean daily maximum is 18.4 °C, and it gets 950mm in annual rainfall. Nearby (50km) is Albury-Wodonga, a regional centre with 74,000 people that straddles the state line.

Kyneton / Daylesford, Victoria

Kyneton (513m), Daylesford (616m), Woodend (580m) & Trentham (700m) surround a diamond-shaped area that is well suited to 2012 survivalism. Just over one hour's drive from the millions of people in Melbourne, these towns have small populations of up to 6,000. The climate is cool, and there are plenty of "weekenders" and "hobby farms" where city folk are trying their hand at country living.

Twenty acres with an existing house can be found for $300-400K. Bare land is cheaper, but if it is less than 100 acres getting a permit to build can be difficult, so make sure a permit is in place. Cheaper land is available to the north of Daylesford.

Be mindful of bush fires, as many properties have uncleared land, or are close to large bush areas. On the other hand, proximity to bush will be useful for applying for a permit to build a "fire" bunker.

If there is a downside, then it is too close to Melbourne. A Melbourne evacuation would occur in many directions; however you'd still want to have a property that is hidden away.

Ballarat / Clunes, Victoria

Just down the road from Daylesford, the triangle between Ballarat, Clunes and Creswick has the same qualifications, but is much cheaper.

This area is where I will be surviving. A huge factor is the proximity to Melbourne – my favorite city in the whole world. If pushed for a figure, I consider the odds of a global catastrophe in 2012 to be about 10-1. Therefore it is important to me that I can maintain my lifestyle whilst still having the insurance of a nearby survival spot.

Rest of Australia

Western Australia is too dry, and those areas that are not are too close to the coast. Also, this is one of the most isolated places in the world, so escape across thousands of miles of deserts could prove to be impossible. The Northern areas of Australia are tropical. Aside from climate change potentially causing it to become unbearably hot, there are also factors such as mosquitoes, disease, and spoiled food. If your southern Australian safe spot ends up being too cold (perhaps it ends up in the South Pole), you can always trek north – one of the major advantages of surviving on a large, flat continent.

New Zealand

Geologically speaking, New Zealand is **not a great place to survive**. Most people live on the coast. One third of all New Zealanders live in Auckland, which is the only major city in the world to have two harbors – that is *really* coastal. To make things worse, Auckland is built on top of many volcanoes that are considered dormant. The most recent volcano is Rangitoto Island at the entrance to Waitemata Harbour, which was only *formed* 1000 years ago. The North Island has many volcanoes, not the least of which is the supervolcano Lake Taupo. Like Japan it is on the Pacific Ring of Fire, and that means earthquakes as well as volcanoes, hence the country's nickname *The Shaky Isles*.

The highest and safest land can be found in the South Island. Although calmer than the North Island, it still gets earthquakes, such as the recent 7.1 in Christchurch, and a 7.8 in Fiordland in 2009.

North Island

For those that choose to live in Auckland, the location of your suburb should determine your safe spot. Those in the south should look further south, and those in the north and west should look north. Major roads in Auckland can get very clogged, and it might prove impossible to travel through the central suburbs if the city is in panic mode.

Kaikohe

Too far for Aucklanders to get to in a hurry, Kaikohe is the "hub of the north", with a population of just 4,000 people, but servicing 28,000. The soil is fertile. Kaikohe itself is not very far above sea level, but it is the most inland you can get north of Auckland (roughly 50kms). The highest peaks in the region are 600-700 meters above sea level, although any achievable safe spot will be much lower. Expect to pay $NZ200K for 10 acres of bare land, or $NZ300K for a few acres with a house.

Just North of Auckland

This area is not ideal for surviving a tsunami, but you need to make do with what is available. At 100kms or less from the northern and western suburbs of Auckland, you should be able to get to (slightly) inland places like **Wellsford** and **Ahuroa** reasonably quickly. Closer to Auckland gets very expensive, the east coast is relatively expensive, and the west coast (South Kaipara Heads) suffers from single road syndrome. Like many places in New Zealand, there's just one road in and out.

I chose Wellsford and Ahuroa on price alone; there are places for sale for not much more than what you'd pay way up in Kaikohe. North of Auckland your key criteria should be price and proximity. Plus, keep in mind that an exodus from Auckland will involve a clogging of SH1 – you are best being well away from the North Island's main highway, and finding somewhere you can get to using lesser roads.

Just South of Auckland

Avoid the Coromandel Peninsula, no matter how much you may like it – the roads are too prone to failure. For a quick escape, look for a spot near Clevedon, a country area west of Manurewa. If nothing around there is affordable, work out an alternative route to bypass SH1, and look at the Paeroa / Te Aroha / Morrinsville / Te Kauwhata quadrangle.

Central North Island

Be wary of single road syndrome – the cheapest properties are understandably more remote, but typically with no alternate ways in or out. A single landslide or bridge outage could render your spot inaccessible. Major downers are the volcanoes of this region. There is nowhere I would recommend until you get as far south as Palmerston North.

Wellington

Don't be in Wellington. There are only two roads out (both prone to being closed), it is on the coast, the weather sucks at the best of times and it sits on top of a major fault line. If you must be there for some reason, at least try and commute from somewhere further north, along State Highway 2, like **Masterton**. Anywhere along SH2 is a great survival spot, as long as you are actually there when the SHTF. Land is cheap and scenic. It isn't very elevated, and the coast is quite near, but for a cost/worthiness ratio I rate it the best area of the North Island.

South Island

There is a lot to like about the South Island – it is cheaper than the North and there are no volcanoes. Outside of the cities it is sparsely populated, but that's because there's not many places suitable for living. Half of the island is taken up by the Southern Alps. A negative is that it is much colder than the North, but at least it is cheaper.

Top of the South Island

In terms of lifestyle and like-minded locals, this is a good place to be. Otherwise, I cannot recommend Blenheim, Nelson or the surrounding area. There isn't much inland, and well, single road syndrome.

Christchurch

Darfield is close to Christchurch, on the train line, has multiple routes in and out, and is quite cheap. The views to the Southern Alps are brilliant. However, this was the epicenter of the 2010 7.1 quake ☹

Otago

This is the best South Island zone. Roxburgh, Alexandra & Cromwell all have cheap land and multiple access points, plus are close to Queenstown if that appeals to you. Further south the same characteristics apply to the triangle of Winton, Gore and Lumsden.

Africa

South Africa

I do not suggest that anyone moves to South Africa for survival purposes, unless they know the place well. The following opinions are only for those who already live there.

The major cities (except for Johannesburg) are coastal. Tsunamis are not really a risk for South Africa – a study conducted after the devastating Asian tsunami of 2004, by a Japanese research group, concludes:

> "The probability of a major tsunami devastating the South Africa coast is very low. However, the consequence of the impact could be catastrophic."

A list of historical tsunamis at Wikipedia does not mention any part of Africa ever being affected, and while that does not mean there has not been any, it seems a whole lot safer than Asia or the Pacific.

Johannesburg is the largest city in the world that is not alongside the coast, a lake or a river. It is also situated 1750m above sea level. While it is safe from flooding, it does have 10 million people and a high existing crime rate. For those reasons alone, this is not somewhere you should choose to be when the SHTF.

Cape Town is (according to some online commentators) the safest major city crime wise, but a big negative is the nearby nuclear power plant, the only one in South Africa. Interestingly, the nation did have a nuclear weapons program, but that was terminated in the early 90s and all weapons were dismantled.

The Drakensberg (literally "Dragon mountains" in Dutch) have long been championed by Patrick Geryl, and their mention at the end of the 2012 movie highlights popularity of the *idea* of surviving there. The mountains have a lot of good features, such as height (up to 3400 meters) and rainfall. Below the tree line (2500m) you can find grassland, woodland and forest. Further down there is an abundance of wildlife, including antelopes, wildebeest and rare white rhinos.

The mountains include parts of Swaziland and Lesotho, places that I think would need to be visited to determine their appropriateness. Geryl has kept secret the precise location of his survival spot, but I'd be looking at the tourist area of **Central Drakensberg**, around Champagne Valley. Specifically Winterton. South Africans should consider visiting this area in late 2012 as a tourist, although thanks to Geryl the area could potentially be booked out for that December. If you come from a prosperous country, the land here might seem to be a bargain. For example in Winterton when I last looked you could buy a lodge within a game reserve (giraffes and zebras as neighbours) for $US280K or a 3-bedroom house with pool for $US140K. A house and 20-50 acres can be obtained for $350K to $750K.

There is also a Buddhist Retreat in nearby Ixopo, where you can stay for long periods for as little as $30/day including food.

The Rest of Africa

Nowhere stands out, and there really isn't enough information online to find any excellent spots. However, the lack of earthquakes and nuclear threats are both strong positives. Whether they are worth being in countries that are (typically) war-torn, corrupt and impoverished is down to the individual. From a purely latitudinal point of view, I have always thought that highlands of **Cameroon** had possibilities, because close to the equator, a crustal pole shift in any direction would be unlikely to be too arduous climate-wise – based on Hapgood's work that suggests pole shifts are typically 30 degrees. **Bamenda** has 400,000 people and is 1600 meters above sea level, with a cool climate. The country is more stable than most of its neighbors. Unfortunately, accompanying the height are some volcanoes – Cameroon is the only west coast nation to have them.

Great Rift Valley is a geological fault system running more than 4000 miles from the Jordan valley in Israel along the Red Sea into Ethiopia, and through Kenya, Tanzania, and Malawi into Mozambique. It is noteworthy for a series of steep-sided lakes such as Lake Turkana, Tanganyika, and Nyasa, as well as a series of volcanoes including Mt. Kilimanjaro. Avoid.

Ethiopia has volcanoes like Erte Ale. The other mountainous regions of East Africa, including Yemen, will probably be overrun by Middle Eastern refugees. The Atlas Mountains will probably be overrun by European refugees.

South America

If, like me, your key criteria involve avoiding volcanoes and earthquakes, then you should basically forget about the west coast of South America. Two of the deadliest earthquakes last century were in Peru (1970, 66,000 people died) and Chile (1939, 29,000 deaths). And the entire length of the coast line has active volcanoes, from Chile to Colombia.

Brazil

Brazil is interesting in that it has some large cities that are a substantial distance from the coast, and with a reasonable climate.

Brasilia is 1000 kilometers inland and 1100 meters above sea level. This purpose-built capital city is modern and relatively prosperous. The governmental nature of Brasilia means that there is a good number of police and armed forces, and these could be beneficial in event of global disorder. The large population (3.6 million people) is a negative, but perhaps balancing that out is that it is within an agricultural region. When the SHTF, this might be one city that survives when cut off from the rest of world.

110 kilometres north of Brasilia a survival community is being planned. It is located near the town of Formosa, above the Salto Itiquira waterfall. It is called Noosphere Technology Center. It is associated with the Citates Resort ecological park and hotel, a place you can stay now for roughly $US100 per night. http://www.citates.com.br

Argentina

My #1 choice for South America is the Cordoba province in Argentina. The city of **Cordoba** has similar attributes to Brasilia – inland, agricultural, pleasant climate. It also has a large student population. The province is popular with tourists – it has 500,000 hotel beds – which means you could choose to visit for Dec 2012 (be aware that Nov-Mar is the rainy season). I am aware of several 2012 survival groups in this area, but I will respect the privacy of their specific locations.

The area comprises of mountains and valleys.

Also consider Chapada Diamantina National Parl in Bahia, Brazil. You can stay in the pretty 19th century town of **Lençóis** which serves as a base camp of sorts. The beauty of this location is the height of 600+ meters, and plentiful rainfall. Locals and visitors are quite likely to be interested in outdoor pursuits, and there are lots of amazing caves and waterfalls. I wouldn't rate it for long-term survival, but it is an interesting and different place to spend December 2012.

North America

There are two maps that could be very relevant to your chances of survival, for few people can survive nuclear radiation or volcanic ash.

The first is from the USGS, showing the ash fallout zones from previous eruptions of Yellowstone. Additionally Long Valley is also on the west coast, so if you think a 2012 event could set off Long Valley or Yellowstone, half of the USA is not suitable.

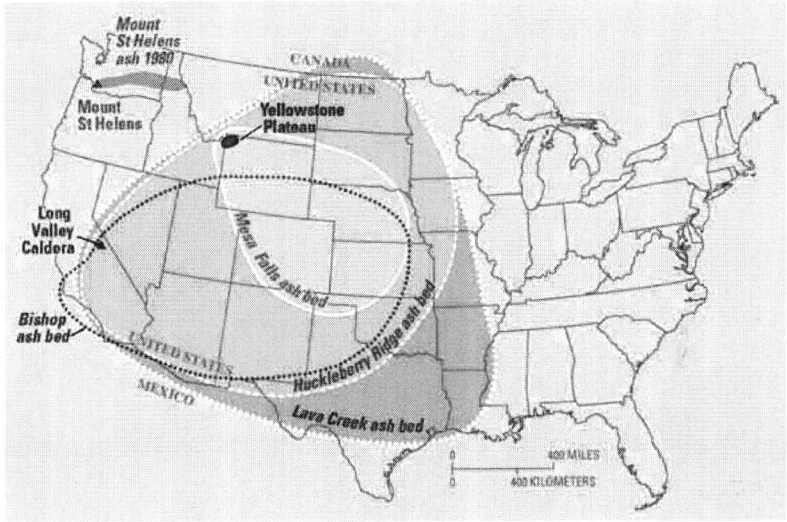

The second is from the NRC and shows nuclear power plants:

U.S. Commercial Nuclear Power Reactors—Years of Operation

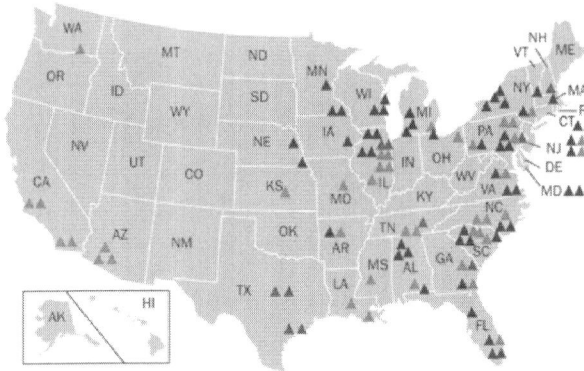

Years of Commercial Operation	Number of Reactors
△ 0-9	0
▲ 10-19	10
▲ 20-29	42
▲ 30-39	52

Source: U.S. Nuclear Regulatory Commission

While the dangers of radiation are scary enough on their own, keep in mind that in the north-east society is dependent on nuclear plants for almost 50% of their electricity. Without them, people in that region are in for a rude awakening.

At first glance, it would seem that with the risks of radiation and ash combined, nowhere in the USA is safe. However, according to FEMA, if you are more than 50 miles from a nuclear power plant you should be safe. Perhaps double it and say 100 miles is safe. This will leave us some pockets away from the west where we can look for a good spot to be.

The third major threat is earthquakes. In this regard virtually all of California will be unsuitable for a safe spot. The other region that could suffer is between Memphis and the southern border of Illinois, known as the New Madrid Fault. Back in the early 1800s this location received a pair of 7.0+ earthquakes and experts have warned it could get hit again, especially with the recent tremors.

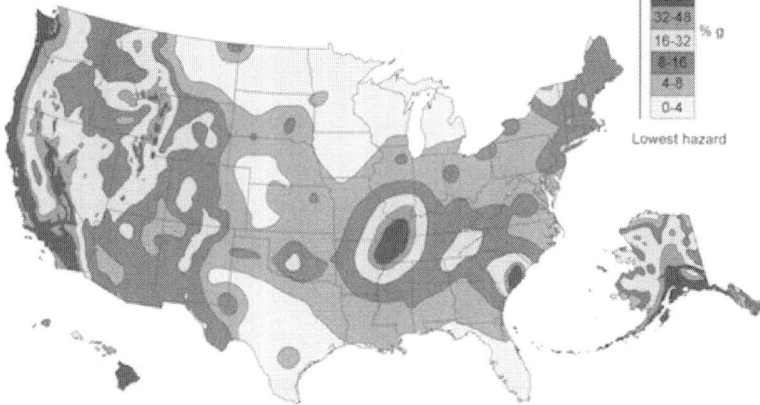

A fourth consideration is population density. As long as you are able to be self-sufficient, being in an area that has less people is highly desirable.

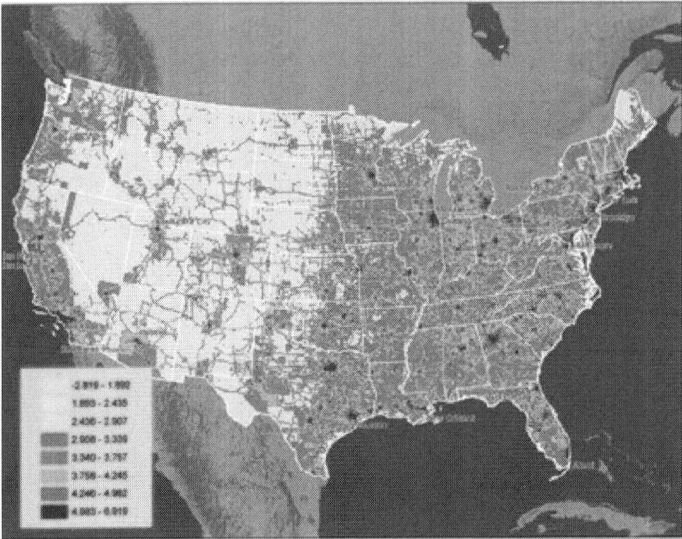

Note that I said less people, not few people. The lighter areas are sparsely populated because they aren't particularly hospitable. You need to be near other people to some extent, and in the worst scenarios larger towns nearby means better scavenging. Based on population alone I'd be choosing mid-to-south central USA.

I'll start off with a region which I believe has the safest survival spots in the USA – East Kentucky and South-East Ohio:

East Kentucky

Kentucky is one of the few states in the eastern half of the USA that does not have nuclear power plants. And virtually all of Kentucky is more than 100 miles away from such facilities. There is a good reason for this; they have coal mines and coal-powered electricity, as well as hydroelectric.

Other positive factors are the distance from the coast, plus the protection from tsunamis provided by the Appalachian Mountains. Very large cities are a long way away, while the state has enough people (4 million) that you aren't too secluded. The weather varies a fair bit, but at least it is not an extreme. Water is in good supply. And the land is fertile enough to grow fruit and vegetables.

Of value to many seeking safe spots is land prices – they are low in this region, so if you were to choose to move here, it is most likely going to be cheaper, or at least on par with your present location. The forests are plentiful, and good for hunting and also for hiding, if need be. Aside from buying some land, you could also consider booking a cabin or camping spot in a forest for late 2013. Several "intentional communities" can be found near Lexington. That's code for groups of self-sufficient hippies.

Here are some towns that stand out:

Corbin – handy to the Daniel Boone State Forest, which has one of the world's largest concentrations of caves. This is excellent for those who don't mind using natural shelters instead of building a bunker. An example of available property is 13 acres with a 2 bedroom cottage for $65,000. Or a 3 bed / 2 bath home on 46 acres for $130,000. It is also home to the Harland Sanders Cafe and Museum, where Col. Sanders perfected his Kentucky Fried Chicken recipe.

Hazard – yep, this town was the inspiration for the Dukes of Hazzard TV series. It is quite remote, and in a heavily-wooded area. The locals do not tend to have much of an income, and the town itself has lost 40% of its population since the middle of last century, dropping from 7,400 to 4,750. This is a good scenario for finding cheap property. In nearby Hueysville I found a trailer home on 33 acres for just $42,000. Be aware that there are some ugly spots around Hazard due to the coal mining.

Berea – buy an acre of clear land for $10K or so. This town was selected by Lawrence E. Joseph in his excellent book Apocalypse 2012, saying *If any place is immune from Apocalypse 2012, it is Berea, Kentucky*. He also points out that it is Christian with a capital C, and a tourist attraction due to all the arts and crafts generated by college students to pay for their tuition. A video on the town as a safe haven is here:
http://www.msnbc.msn.com/id/26184891/vp/34651447#34651447

Louisville – Mega Cavern. I would move to Louisville for this, but folk in Kentucky & Indiana or Cincinnati should also be aware of this marvelous facility. It is located under and near the Louisville Zoo, and consists of 100 acres of underground caverns, the remains of limestone mining. It is privately owned, and space is let out to various businesses. During the Cold War the US government designated the cavern as a nuclear shelter capable of holding 50,000 people. To take a look at the cavern, they run guided tours (http://www.louisvillemegacavern.com). The web site for the commercial storage aspect is at www.louisvilleunderground.com. Storing a trailer or RV starts at $75/mo. Fill it with supplies, and anytime you are worried you can go to your trailer, which happens to be in the safest place in Louisville!

South East Ohio

The southern half of Ohio is also more than 100 miles from any nuclear power plant (although there once was a uranium processing plant at Fernald, just outside of Cincinnati). Land is cheap, and of interest to many 2012ers is that it has some ancient monuments. For camping, Wisteria (www.wisteria.org) is an excellent choice for anyone who has New Age or pagan leanings.

Chillicothe – as the centre of the ancient Hopewell tradition, nearby you will find the Hopewell Culture National Historic Park, with dozens of earthen mounds. Only 20,000 people, and on a major highway – yet there are many other alternate routes in and out. TV survivalism expert Dave Canterbury is from here. Properties available in early 2011 included a 3 bedroom house on 5 acres with some great shedding for $120,000, or a shack on 2 acres in the woods for $40,000. For camping in Dec 2012, try nearby Tar Hollow State Park.

Peebles, Ohio is my <u>#1 safe spot</u> for all of the USA.

With a population of just 1700 people, Peebles is classified as a village. But if you need a city Cincinnati is just an hour's drive away. Property is great value relative to the coastal states - you can buy 20 acres of cleared land for $40,000.

Just 5 miles north of the town is the famous Great Serpent Mound. It is roughly 1000 years old, 411 meters long, and is the largest snake effigy in the world. Many 2012ers will already have heard of this historic landmark and perhaps wished to visit it. Interestingly, State geologists concluded in 2003 that a meteorite once crashed into the site.

For the last 9 years the Friends of Serpent Mound have held a *Lighting the Serpent* event on the winter solstice, and presumably it will be held on Dec 21, 2012. On that evening they place and then light 900 candles, as a well as a sacred fire.

Cabins (from $70 per night) and camping (from $23 per night) are available at Long's Retreat. There's also Mineral Springs Lake Resort (which has some pretty dire reviews) and if you like getting completely back to nature, the Cedar Trails Nudist Retreat (although it is only open from May to September).

The Amish are well-known for their back-to-basics culture, and Peebles has almost 100 Amish households. While they are not known for socializing with outsiders, they do trade and are typically pacifists – so having so many living locally can only be a plus, post-SHTF.

The Ten Biggest US Metro Areas

These cities are so large that the #1 priority is getting out ahead of the pack. It doesn't matter how close or good your safe spot is if you cannot get to it. In general the following suggestions do not account for traffic, or your personal location within the city.

San Francisco / San Jose

Hopefully you don't live in downtown San Francisco, because that could prove to be a difficult place to escape from. I'd forget the bridges and head south along the coast.

For everyone else, head for Sacramento, then get past Sacramento on the east side. The safe spot I recommend is **Grass Valley**, a pleasant former gold-mining community with lots going on. This fulfils another safe spot criteria – visiting your spot can be a vacation, not a chore. A home in the hills, private with a few acres, can be purchased for $100K-$200K. If yoga is your thing, check out the local Sivananda Ashram Yoga Farm.

Normally I would look for somewhere further away from major cities, but east has rough terrain, west has a famous fault line, south has many people, and north has a dam that could burst (Shasta Dam). Be very careful to make sure your safe spot, anywhere in the world, is not below a dam. Dams can break in earthquakes, and overflow with heavy rain / change of climate / lack of engineers.

Los Angeles / San Diego

A key factor in many scenarios is the San Andreas fault, which runs through San Francisco, down the Pacific coast, alongside the San Bernardino mountains and down the middle of the Gulf of California. Ideally you want to be east of this fault line before a major earthquake occurs. This will mean you are safe from the earthquake, and roads/bridges are still passable. Best case scenario from L.A. or San Diego would be 1-2 hours of driving to get beyond the fault line. After that, plan on a lot more driving, because southern California is too arid, and not recommended for survival.

Exiting the city is very important for L.A., so I would aim to get to **Barstow**, a major highway hub, and have a safe spot somewhere way beyond. Many L.A. folk might think of the road to Las Vegas when escape is required, but fortunately there are alternate routes to Barstow. But once you reach Barstow, do not head towards Vegas, and do not contemplate surviving in Vegas – it will be like a refugee camp.

A good move would be to buy a property in or around Barstow. A house can be purchased for less than $30,000, which means a deposit as low as $1000, and repayments of about $1000/yr. Or you could rent a property, or even a lockup. While it would be OK to survive here for short-term events, the key is that you have a supply cache in Barstow, a place where you can store fuel, food & water, as a waypoint towards somewhere better, such as Flagstaff.

Albuquerque, New Mexico is 8-9000 feet above sea level, which some survivalists find appealing. Being so far inland, height is not a necessity, and you'll find that the arid climate and inability to grow crops major negatives for many SHTF scenarios, such as a loss of the power grid, or a pandemic. I recommend heading farther east.

San Diego

Considering you would not head towards Los Angeles, San Diego has two ways out – south of the border and east. East is preferable, but Baja California is an option for those who like the area and are familiar with it. Obviously you would not want to drive through Tijuana, but rather skirt around it.

Blythe is similar to Barstow, as it is a traffic hub with low property prices. My suggestion is to have a cache in Blythe.

While Flagstaff is nice, and Sedona has appeal to many, for long term survival you want to head much further east. Beyond Texas you will find it easier to live off the land, as opposed to the dry regions approaching Texas. For those worried about nuclear fallout, there happens to be a reasonably wide corridor – typically 100+ miles – that is a safe distance from any nuclear facilities. It follows the Texas/Oklahoma border (don't plan on crossing Red River), then along southern Arkansas, up through northern Mississippi, and then western Tennessee to Kentucky and finally southern West Virginia. Along this path it is quite easy to keep away from major cities, access/scavenge supplies and get to anywhere that suits you, pre-determined or otherwise.

Houston / Dallas

Without a doubt, if you do not have a local safe spot, north-east is the direction to head, following the path detailed above. For a local safe spot, consider:

Hemphill, TX – out-of-the-way, where the Sabine National Forest meets the Toledo Bend Reservoir. Expensive for a safe spot, homes will set you back $100K+. However, if your family desires a vacation home, then this could serve a dual-purpose.

Mena, AR – servicing the Ouachita Mountains, Mena is a place people visit for the outdoor activities. Only 150 miles from Dallas, prices are very good. A quick search at Trulia.com found an acre of bare land for $12,000, 4 acres for $22,500, and a one-bedroom home for $18,000. There's some elevation as well, the city is 357 meters above sea level. Population of 5000.

Further afield is Whitwell, TN (see below)

Atlanta

In my opinion the Chattanooga, TN area makes for an excellent choice, and you can get there in less than 3 hours. The city is surrounded by mountains and ridges, and it is affordable with great livability. Just outside of Chattanooga is **Whitwell**. Small parcels of land, or homes, can be found for under $25,000 if you aren't too fussy. The Sequatchie Valley Institute teaches sustainability, and has a few places for interns – meaning you can live there for $5-$10/day.

On the other side of Chattanooga, within the Chattahoochee National Forest is a town called Hiawassee. There you will find **Enota** – which has turned the most elevated private land in Georgia into a working farm and RV site. Park your RV at their "Entrepreneurial Village" for $1000/mo, which includes T1 internet connections. With or without your own RV, you can also stay for free in exchange for work.

Note: Chattanooga is listed as having a risk of earthquakes by the USGS, however it is at the bottom of the scale, and nothing like the New Madrid zone or California.

Chicago or Detroit or Minneapolis

North-Eastern US cities offer two general directions: trek south to Kentucky and West Virginia, or have a safe spot to the North, just before or in Canada. Heading north has a major problem – cold weather and snow. Unless you are certain that climate change will be in your favor, the winters will mean your survival is substantially more difficult.

The Upper Peninsula of Michigan holds minor appeal, due to the sparse population, the ease of getting there from Minneapolis and Chicago, and cheap prices. But unless you get lucky due to some cataclysm-created climate change, it is too cold to consider.

Heading south, there are no obvious safe spots. Kentucky, West Virginia and Tennessee are a long drive, especially if you are caught unprepared. Having a mid-point cache would be prudent if you have the dollars and inclination. When choosing a cache location, secondary considerations are accessibility in a crisis, costs, familiarity, and an x-factor that makes you like the location. Of primary importance is that you can get there. Even if you strive to keep your gas tank full, honestly how low does it sometimes get? That's how close your cache needs to be.

If you typically refuel when your tank is half empty, and that gets you 150 miles, then your cache needs to be that close. That way, if you are at a party, or work, or a picnic, or a ball game, and you are alerted somehow, and going home first is not an option, you can get to your cache. Your cache will have everything you need (fuel, food, water etc) to get you to your safe spot further south.

Nowhere has special appeal for me in Indiana, but at a push I'd offer **Bloomington** and surrounds. But only if you know you'll have the gas to get there!

(If you do choose Bloomington for a cache, check out the (failed) reproduction of the Great Pyramid in nearby Bedford.)

New York City / Boston

The famous **Woodstock** is just two hour's drive from NYC, and if you can afford it, makes an ideal safe spot. Nearby **Cairo** is more affordable. And it gets cheaper the further inland you head. Near Liberty I found a 2 bedroom home on 5 acres for $30K.

If you live in New York City, getting out when the SHTF could prove difficult, if not impossible, because the few bridges and tunnels that cross the Hudson River will become jammed. And depending on the scenario, they might not be safe either. Furthermore, in the event of a terrorist attack/threat, or act of war, tunnels and bridges could be closed by the authorities. They were closed to all except emergency vehicles for 24 hours or more following the 9/11 attacks.

Unless you have a bunker in the Hamptons, north will be the direction to head. For my recommended safe spots, at some stage you will need to cross the Hudson. Although bridges further north are less likely to be blocked/closed, there could still be a significant amount of escaping traffic, and bridges might not withstand the force of whatever is occurring. If you have the basic skills, consider crossing by boat. This means having a boat stored safely away at your preferred crossing point, and having a cache on the other side of the river.

I think the best crossing point would be near Rip Van Winkle Bridge. The bridge has a pedestrian walkway, which means you could also beat the traffic jam with a motorcycle. For a boat crossing, the river is about 1500ft wide here, and 10 miles north it is only 600ft wide.

While the areas near to Rip Van Winkle Bridge do not have many bargain properties, you could also consider a self-storage facility – but make sure you can access your storage in an emergency.

One such facility in **Leeds** (walking distance from Rip Van Winkle Bridge) has suitable "drive up" storage units, large enough to fit a car, for $110-$135 per month. Keep a vehicle here, loaded with supplies and fuel. Drive to the bridge from Boston or NYC (consider a motorcycle if you live in NYC), and if you can't drive across the bridge you can walk across it.

Even better, drive a pickup or wagon and keep an inflatable dinghy in it. A four-person dinghy can be purchased for less than $1000 including a foot pump.

When you retrieve your fully-stocked vehicle from your Leeds storage facility, head to your local safe spot, or head south. Specifically, west then south. If it were me, I would risk the long travel and have a spot in Ohio or Kentucky, rather than face the harsh winters of the northern states.

Philadelphia / Washington D.C.

This part of the USA is very populated and doesn't offer much for survivalists. I suggest fleeing west. Because many others could have the same idea, pay particular attention to your exit routes. While freeways are going to get you out quickest, traffic can be a problem. Every step of the way you need to be aware of which secondary roads will serve you best. There are enough of these to ensure that everyone who considers leaving the major arteries should be able to escape.

My favored region of East Kentucky and South-East Ohio is probably beyond the range of your vehicle. If this is the case, you will either need to carry spare fuel in your vehicle at all times, or have a cache midway.

Midway covers a large area, depending on your starting point and your chosen roads. Land isn't particularly cheap, and there are no stand-out locations. If pushed I'd suggest Parsons, WV, or Altoona, PA.

Your best bet is to utilize a self storage facility. 10 feet by 15 feet, with drive up access, can be had for $120-$130 in **Frederick, MD**. This town is easy to access, and just 150 miles from Philadelphia, or 50 miles from Washington DC. There you can keep a vehicle, fuel, and supplies sufficient to complete your escape.

Miami / Fort Lauderdale

Williston, FL is about the right distance from Miami for a cache. If you can get out of the cities, then a place that has your extra supplies (especially fuel / water / food) is very useful to have. If you just grab supplies and keep going, that is great. Or you can stay until the panic has subsided – depending on the scenario of course. A run down home or trailer on a small lot can be had for under $20,000. A bargain I noticed during my research was a 3 bed/2 bath home on 1.25 acres, hidden away behind trees, with a large pole barn, for $28,000.

Otherwise, I have not yet discovered a standout safe-spot between Miami and Chattanooga.

Always keep in mind, the best spot is **one you will actually use** – so for most people that means being within a few hour's drive of your home. A second-rate survival spot in the hand is worth two in the bush! Find the best compromise for your situation.

Canada

In general, your options are staying put or making a major journey southwards. Every survivalist should aim for having a few years' worth of food stored away, but if winters in your area are a significant factor, then food and shelter are critical. For most Canadians I do not recommend seeking out a local safe spot – you'll be better served by improving the survivability of your home.

Eastern Canada

The major cities of eastern Canada all suffer the problem of very cold winters. I can only suggest fleeing south to the USA. *Or staying at home.*

One of my blog readers asked about how best to survive if you live on Prince Edward Island. Staying at home is an option for her, because the island can support agriculture. I'd be recommending the island to people of Ottawa, Montreal and Quebec if it was connected to the mainland, instead of relying on a long narrow bridge.

British Columbia

My advice for Vancouver also applies to Portland and Seattle in the USA. You are so isolated that I'd plan on staying put. I could not find any towns or areas that stand out as places to be. If you have a favorite local getaway, or you have friends or family on a farm, then they'd be good options. But I wouldn't invest heavily in a safe spot – instead use any funds you have to build up your supplies at home. Rent some local storage space if need be.

Europe

Besides all that I list below, <u>consider an overseas vacation for Dec 2012</u>. Consider Australia. Being there with just a suitcase will probably be a better option that anywhere in Europe – unless you have the funds to buy land and install a bunker within a few hours' drive of where you live.

Otherwise, head for the hills!

Seriously, the UK and Europe are very crowded places, and can be quite expensive. Finding a remote 20 acre block and building a shelter or bunker is much harder than in the Americas, Australasia or Africa. Ultimately the only places that are relatively safe and free of people will be the hills. Your budget will determine whether that means buying land, using a lockup, caching or having supplies in your car boot. But the place to go will be the hills.

The good news is that getting to the hills should be easy if you plan in advance. Roads are everywhere, and for most of Europe at each junction you will have many route choices. If you avoid motorways, grid locks are unlikely to be a problem, and any hindrances should be easy to circumvent.

England and Wales

There are many nice places to have a holiday in England. Lots of castles, camping grounds... The following suggestions might not seem so special, but they are. If the SHTF, they will have the least people, and your best chances of surviving, with or without your own property.

Escaping London

The hardest part will be getting beyond the Ring Road – good luck, or two-wheeled transport, might be needed if you live in the centre of London. Of the many different directions you could head, my suggestion is **Central Wales**.

The best route will be via the Chiltern Hills and Cotswolds. These are relatively higher above sea level, and less populated. If you can afford it, these two areas would be OK to build a top-notch safe spot. Even so, Wales is better. To get there you'll probably need supplies, especially if you forget to keep you fuel tank full. Worthy of consideration is using a self-storage facility. A good example is Fort Lock Self Storage in Banbury (storage-banbury.com). They are budget-minded and have drive-up storage with 24/7 access.

Because you can, work out a dozen different routes to Central Wales, avoiding major cities. And for each route, note any caravan parks. These could prove to be a handy resource if you cannot complete the journey to your safe spot.

Clever Tip: In Dec 2012, most British camping grounds will be closed. Many will have cabins, and of course facilities. If anyone is in charge, there's a good chance they will let you stay if you reward them somehow. But the key would be to get there first, before others think of it.

Quantock Hills, Somerset

Bare in some places, beautiful rolling pastures in others, the Quantock Hills are not well known. This is a big plus. Although quite near the coast, this part of the Bristol Channel should be safe from any tsunami. Rural properties are reasonably priced. From the top of the hills there are also excellent views, as far as Exmoor, Glastonbury and Wales – good for seeing what is going on with a telescope.

The Quantock Orchard Caravan Park has static caravans for around £25,000. Of just hire one for around £50 per night, sleeps 4. They are open all year round, and seem to also have backpacker facilities.

All around the base of the hills you will find mansions, leased out for weddings and so on. Any of these could make for a good emergency refuge if a solid structure is needed. One, Crowcombe Court, is up for sale and not taking bookings. Nice if you have a spare £2 million. Otherwise within walking distance of the mansion is the Carew Arms pub, stay there in Dec 2012 for £50 per night and drink some real ales – perhaps the person with the mansion keys will be there too?

Similarly, Dunster Castle is down by the coast, about eight miles from the Quantock Hills. It is a full-on castle with turrets and dungeons, and is in good shape. Below it is the Dunster Castle Hotel. Above it is Gallox Hill (height 174 metres).

Central Wales / Powys

Powys is easily the least populated county in England and Wales. It is also high up, reasonably accessible, relatively cheap and the land is suitable for self-sufficiency. My personal preference is the rural areas west of **Welshpool**. It is only one hour from Birmingham, so that is perfect if you live there. As an alternative, consider around **Rhayader**.

I will keep on reiterating that the best option is to own your own land. Apart from all the usual SHTF scenarios, if law and order is maintained, you will have a place that is safe and <u>yours</u>. If you don't own where you are staying, you can be asked to leave. If you are able to own rural land in Central Wales, your choices might still be limited, so don't be too fussy.

For everyone else, your choices are squatting (not so bad if few people have survived), seeking charity (*please Sir, can I stay in your barn*), or renting.

And caravan parks, which I keep returning to. They have facilities, they are relatively cheap, and they tend to be rural or semi-rural. As I have noted, many will be closed in the winter of 2012/2013, especially in areas that normally receive snowfall. But some have on-site caravans and cabins that you can buy!

For example, Riverbend Caravan Park near Welshpool has a 2-bedroom Atlas Dakota Super, 32 feet long, for just under £10,000, amongst their six for sale. If you can get a bank loan, and re-sell it after 2012 doesn't happen, your outlay will be modest.

Naughty Tip: Just one mile from Welshpool is Powis Castle. It is a substantial and solid building. While in the long-term you are bound to be usurped (unless you are already part of an armed group), during any SHTF event it could provide the type of shelter you need to survive. Even if hundreds of people think the same way, there will be enough room.

Nottingham / Birmingham

My recommendation is to head to Central Wales. If you prefer, the Lake District is also quite good, but getting there will be more difficult.

Manchester / Liverpool / Sheffield / Leeds

It comes down to traffic. In a SHTF scenario major roads of this belt of cities could become clogged in every direction, with people trying to get out but not having any concrete plans. Head north to the Lake District or south to Central Wales, depending on what the traffic will allow.

Lake District

Generally speaking, if you find a spot in England that is remote and quiet, it won't be a very good survival spot. Cold, wind-swept moors are good for walks and heather, but not for self-sufficiency. Also, flat un-forested areas are not very suitable for hiding!

Within the Lake District is **Grizedale Forest**, and there are also pockets of wooded areas around Lake Windermere, andKeswick as well. If you have New Age leanings, checkout the Castlerigg Stone Circle near Keswick – to me it feels like a good spot to watch the end of the world from.

Grizedale Camping (grizedale-camping.co.uk) has budget camping at £6 per person, plus wooden huts that sleep four for £25/night. This place is ideal for those who want to go somewhere safe just for the week surrounding Dec 21. And it is open all-year-round.

If buying a static caravan appeals, when I looked Wild Rose and Skiddaw View both had some for under £20,000.

Worth consideration are the bushcraft courses run by Woodsmoke, who are based near Hawkshead. Instead of dismissing your chances of surviving a doomsday, take a course and get a feel for it. For the rest of your life (2012 willing) you can take your normal holidays, but this year, try a survivalist course. *I dare you.*

Scotland

The best general safe spot area is easy – **Perthshire**. The population is relatively low, the land is fertile, and the hills are accessible. Narrowing it down further, I'd be looking at the area surrounding **Blairgowrie**, and perhaps Dunkeld. In between, at the tiny town of Caputh, is an independent backpacker's hostel, a bargain at £18 per night. Otherwise the district has caravan parks, hotels and even mansions available to rent on a weekly basis. As far as I can tell, buying a worthwhile survival spot in this region would not be possible for most people.

As with London, the biggest challenge for most Scots is escaping the Glasgow/Edinburgh population corridor. Edinburgh locals should avoid the Forth of Firth bridge and head north via Stirling.

Alternatively, and especially if escaping north looks like too much of a challenge, consider the south-west of **Galloway Forest Park**, around Loch Ken, Castle Douglas and Haugh of Orr. It doesn't have much in height, but is safe from tsunamis. And I'd expect the area will remain quiet when the SHTF. There are several independent backpacker hostels, and excellent camping at Marthrown of Mabie or the Galloway Activity Centre.

Lastly, if you are like me and fancy your chances storming a castle while the rest of the world are panicking, between Crieff and Gleneagles there are some excellent castles. (Conspiracy theorists might note that the Bilderberg Group met at Gleneagles in 1986).

Continental Europe

To put it bluntly, the north is too cold, and the south is too prone to earthquakes. So really you should be heading for the middle. A major potential problem is crossing borders. In a catastrophe borders could be closed, so it is imperative that you work out in advance (that means now), roads you can take that are less likely to be blocked.

Aside from borders, Europe is massively complicated to summarize. At this stage I am not able to provide recommendations for every large city. Hopefully this will not be a problem, because you can use my criteria to work out your best safe spot:

- Low population
- Won't come to mind when people panic and flee populated areas
- Not near a major thoroughfare / road
- Elevated if near the coast
- Away from fault lines, nuclear reactors and volcanoes
- Fertile land
- New Age locals

Best direction is *towards* the **Alsace region** of France that borders Germany. Wherever you are in Europe, in general heading for that region will give you the best compromise between earthquakes and cold. Alsace itself is not great, it is highly populated, is along a border, is along a river. And it is in the middle of the densest region of nuclear reactors in Europe.

To avoid nukes, aim for Switzerland, **Dijon**, or the border between Germany and the Czech Republic. As I have mentioned in other chapters, a lack of nukes typically means a lack of population, so that is win-win. All around Dijon looks good, and between Dresden and Prague looks excellent as well.

Switzerland

Switzerland is difficult to get to. Unless you live really close, it's a non-starter. But if you can get there, or live there, the whole country is a bunker. While many are decrepit or repurposed, during the Cold War the Swiss government made sure that there was a bunker space for every man, woman and child. So if you are Swiss, stay put. The south and east of the country are free from nuclear power plants.

Eastern Europe

For those in Western Europe, one of the features of Eastern Europe is that it is a relatively cheap place to visit. Poland, and the Baltic countries to its north, are far less likely to have a major earthquake than the Mediterranean countries. They also have no nuclear power plants at present, and they are safe from tsunamis. Unless you lived in Germany, Russia or Belarus I wouldn't be constructing a Baltic bunker or safe spot, but it is appealing for a Dec 2012 vacation.

Polish Ski Holiday

There are some ski resorts in the Krkonoše mountains, such as Karpacz and Szklarska Poręba where you might consider vacationing in Dec 2012. They are better located and cheaper than those to the east. Even better is Kaszuby near Gdansk, get rooms in this scenic location from just $30 per night.

Castles

Some Eastern European castles have hotel type accommodation within their solid walls.

In Latvia there is Jaunpils Castle, Birini Castle and Jaunmoku Pils. They are not terribly expensive, for example Jaunmoku starts at $80.

There are quite a few in Poland, see them at http://hhpolska.com/en

Section 4 – Survival Tips and Tricks

Achieving a Safe Spot

Once you have found a location that suits you, the next step is to make it a reality. Sometimes a tiny amount of effort is all that is required to give you the momentum you need. For example, I was once on a TV game show. The difference between having that experience, or not, was writing my name and address on the back of an envelope and posting it. When the application form arrived, I felt compelled to complete it. When they gave me an interview, I felt compelled to attend. The hardest part was sending the original envelope.

For you the step that gives you momentum might be to phone a realtor and ask if there are any suitable properties for you to look at. Or perhaps filling your car with fuel and driving there, and staying the night. Once you have had a look around, and have chatted to some locals, you could be on your way.

It doesn't matter if you have no money, you still have options. Find cheap, friendly accommodation in the area and make a booking for a few weeks in December 2012. That is certainly better than saying you can't afford to buy a safe spot and giving up.

Thankfully the internet makes looking for real estate (and other things) easy. Take time to search for all possible safe spots. Look at bare land, land with old buildings, land you can build on. Look for rental accommodation, shared accommodation, motels, caravan parks and so on. Search for "intentional communities". There are many such places (often known as communes) which are not specifically for 2012, but are sympathetic towards it.

Look for signs of the type of people that live in your safe area – for example organic farming indicates a more self-sufficient community. Look for employment – perhaps a job comes with accommodation. Perhaps WWOOFing suits? Doing some WWOOFing (working on organic farms) now could provide you with valuable contacts and knowledge.

Mapping Your Options

Google Maps is great for this. Follow the instructions here to build your own customized map, where you can highlight locations and draw routes:
http://maps.google.com/support/bin/answer.py?hl=en&answer=14 4363&topic=1687289

And make sure to print out your final maps!

Food and Water

Drinking water should always be your number one priority, because the lack of it will kill you.

James Wesley Rawles suggests printing out instructions for the use of hypochlorite tablets, and filling zip lock bags with six ounces of the tablets each. You will then be able to quickly dispense them to anyone you come across, and know that your foresight could save lives.

There are a couple of aspects to survival nutrition which tend to be neglected. Meat from the likes of wild rabbits is very lean, and to avoid digestive problems you need to compliment it with fibrous foods, like wheat or corn, or fresh fruit and vegetables. Freshly grown sprouts will do the trick. The other aspect to be aware of is fats and oils. In the west we tend to avoid these as much as possible if we are watching our weight, but your body requires them to some degree.

Bulk survival foods tend to be light on fats, so make sure you have some stored away. Keep plenty of olive oil on hand, make sure you rotate it, and keep an eye on expiry dates. Freezing it is an option, but only in plastic bottles. Other possibilities include canned butter or lard – something to spread on your homemade bread. Also consider mayonnaise, peanut butter or even Spam (which is 27% fat). Aside from stored items, you could also plan on growing peanuts, olives or sunflowers – or raise your own cows/sheep/pigs.

MREs

Meals, Ready to Eat are designed for the armed forces, for men who need to be highly mobile and have high calorific needs. MREs are expensive. The only place for them is in your go bag.

Triple Redundancy

Plans can fall apart or outright fail. This is especially the case where the SHTF scenario might not be the one you most envisage, and could even be something you had never considered.

We are not used to having Plan Bs and Plan Cs in our day-to-day lives. Mostly because we can get by without having other options pre-planned. Partly because it hasn't crossed our minds. Hands up who has a second job/career already planned in case you lose your current job? Even nuclear power plants are guilty of not being prepared for the worst. Most nuclear power plants only have a single backup plan to save them from a meltdown – if the external power supply is cut, they turn on diesel generators. They do not have a reliable Plan C for if the generators fail. That was the problem in Japan in 2011.

However, when it comes to the lives of you and your family, I suggest that you have some spare plans, just in case. If you agree with me that escaping the city when the SHTF is the best option, what will you do if escape isn't possible? Say your car fails to start due to an EMP attack. Or you break your leg during an earthquake? The next best plan is to stay at home (an environment where you have a lot of inside knowledge), BUT to also have prepared for this eventuality. Even if you have a big stash of supplies at your safe spot, keep a good level at home as well.

For Plan C you need to be more creative. Near your home, on route to your safe spot, and near your safe spot, you need alternative survival venues for when your home and safe spot are unavailable to you (say they burned to the ground during a meteor strike...). Here are some ideas to get you thinking:

- Friends/relatives
- Abandoned buildings
- Buildings that will be abandoned when the SHTF, like a sporting pavilion
- Commercial properties with basements
- Commercial properties with supplies, like food distributors
- For those in Europe... a castle!

Obviously you will not have a stash of supplies at such locations, so make sure your B.O.B (bug out bag) is fully equipped.

Emergency Training

Survivalism is a counter-cultural hobby for many, and there's nothing wrong with that. But that doesn't mean you have to ignore orthodox channels of training. Aside from reading books and joining online forums, there are places where you can learn firsthand, from experts, such as:

- Red Cross – learn First Aid
- Army Reserve
- FEMA / Civil Defence courses
- Volunteer Fire Brigade

In his book *Emergency*, Neil Strauss joins a variety of organizations where he learns how to act in an emergency situation. While this is good preparation for solo surviving, where the confidence that you have the appropriate skills is a powerful asset – he is now also more able to help others, *and* he gets to hear about an emergency prior to the general public.

Know Your Safe Spot Neighbours

At home, and at your safe spot, the more people who know (and like you), the better. If you are knocking on someone's door, wanting help during an emergency, how will you be received as a stranger, compared to if you are an acquaintance? Keep in mind that this swings both ways, and you might have neighbors seeking help from you. If being friendly suits you, make an effort to get to know your neighbors, but be very careful to not let on that you have nine rifles, a thousand rounds of ammo and five year's supply of food and water. Soon the whole local district could know.

Consider keeping a database of people in your neighborhood. I don't mean soap opera details, but anything that might be meaningful in a survival scenario. Where do the local doctors live? Who has the same model vehicle as yours (spare parts)? Or, who is old and frail and might be needing your help?

At your safe spot, make a map of the surrounding properties, and get a feel of where the boundaries lie, and who owns what. List their phone numbers – perhaps before fleeing a bush fire you can ask your neighbor how things are looking on their property...

Electric and Electronic Items

If the power grid is down, possibly down forever, then you'll need electricity for your devices. At your survival spot a generator is a must, and the native output of your generator should be DC. Using an inverter is relatively inefficient, so to conserve future energy buy electrical products that can run on DC power wherever possible.

For batteries, products that take the standard sizes are a significantly better choice than ones that take obscure battery sizes. Even though they might expire before you get to use them, buying hundreds of batteries today could be a smart investment. Batteries sold at your local 7/11 are 2x, 4x or even 10x more expensive than bulk purchases. A Google search for "buy bulk batteries" will find stores that sell them from about 50c each. eBay is another good place to try. If you are wanting to buy hundreds of batteries, batteryjunction.com has AA Duracell Coppertops for 25c each. Even if you only use a fraction of those purchased, you will have saved money compared with buying them from a convenience store at the last minute. And when the SHTF, they will likely be one of the new currencies.

Mechanical Items and Tools

It doesn't really matter what they are used for, if you have the opportunity, accumulate them. Anything a builder or mechanic or farmer would use, is going to be valuable post-SHTF. Buy anything in this category that you feel you will need personally, and if you come across anything else (yard sales, friends throwing old equipment away), grab it.

Unusual or Unexpectedly Useful Items

Here's an assortment of items that are not that obvious, and don't typically turn up on other lists you may come across:

Wet wipes / wet ones / moist towelettes... a very convenient way of cleaning something if there is no water around. Indispensible if you have a baby to care for.

Toiletries and feminine hygiene. Post-SHTF could be a very grubby environment, and in modern society that repulses many of us. These could become luxury items, and help members of your party stay sane.

Engine Oil. Everyone will have canisters of gasoline, but engines need oil as well.

Lime – for makeshift toilets. Buy large bags of it.

Down Jackets, woolen hats, thermal socks, thermal underwear – in case 2012 is the year the next mini-Ice Age begins.

Parachute Cord and Duct Tape are extremely versatile. As one example, imagine how much easier building a bivouac would be with these two items and a good knife.

Spices – compact, cheap, and can make those survival rations taste a lot nicer.

Candle wax and wicking – for when all the batteries have run out.

Dental instruments and supplies (try eBay). Post SHTF, people will still need dentists. If you happen to locate a dentist, he or she might not have any equipment, especially if they have fled the city. Alternatively, armed with the famous *Where There Is No Dentist* book, the instruments can be used by DIY dentists.

Hiding Out

Here's a description of my *ideal* and *specific* safe spot.

- Fifteen minutes drive from a small town, an hour's drive from a large town.
- Uphill, and preferably near the top of a hill. But not so that your property forms part of the skyline...
- At the end of the road. Be able to see (with a telescope or binoculars, and from a lookout, not a house window) all the premises that are along your road. Any unwelcome visitors will probably systematically visit your neighbours, and you'll be last. If you are serious about security, you will see strangers before they see you.

- A bridge that can be destroyed, or a narrow pass than can be caved in. As long as you know of an alternate route, taking out the main route could be a sufficient hindrance to have visitors turn around and look for somewhere more accessible to raid. Or even just fell a tree – most visiting vehicles will not attempt to clear the road unless they are *certain* of something worthwhile ahead.
- Land (and climate) suitable for growing crops and raising livestock.
- Dams, springs, rivers or streams for water. Make sure a once-in-a-hundred-years flood will not affect you.
- Two residences, neither visible from the road.
- The residence closest to the road is the decoy. You will leave it looking like the owners fled a long time ago. That means leaving many things that are too bulky to transport – even if you'd rather be using them in your main house. Let food rot in the refrigerator. Leave the lawnmower in the garage, and so on.
- Your second residence should be as far away from the first as possible, with no obvious means of access. Any existing paths should be disguised or repurposed – perhaps turn a driveway into an (untended) veggie patch.

Ideal, and achievable, but if you manage to tick every box you are fortunate. It might be too arduous to keep your survival home looking like it is uninhabited, but there are a few tricks to keeping your treasures safe from looters...

Hiding Things

Repurpose a bulky object by ripping out the insides to create storage space. Possibilities include tube TVs, computers (if they are worthless post-SHTF), old mattresses (stored vertically in case someone wants a quick nap), or fridges and freezers as long as they are outside and surrounded by overgrown grass. You can use filing cabinets or cardboard boxes as long as you label them so they appear to contain boring useless things like magazines or tax records, and make sure that the first boxes they open actually contain those things.

If you don't have these sorts of old items, get them for free via Freecycle.

Another idea is to bury you items underneath anything you have a pile of, be it firewood, sand, gravel, bricks or hay. Many of your valuable goods can be buried in the ground. The trick is to bury them beneath something that can disguise that "this dirt was recently dug" look. Park a wrecked trailer over your stash, or perhaps a compost bin or a chicken coop.

Also, I mentioned above that you should be able to see your neighbors, but at the same time you do not want your house to be visible. The easiest way to achieve this is via a natural screen. A row of fast growing trees could do the trick, but you need to make sure that the spacing looks natural – try having them more than one row deep.

Sandbags and Gravel

Another great tip from James Wesley Rawles. Ever wondered where all the sandbags come from during a flood emergency? The authorities have them stockpiled, tens of thousands of them, because they are such a useful asset. You can fill them with just about anything, and they are of a size that most able-bodied adults can handle. They stack easily. And they are dirt cheap – when buying in bulk you can get several for a dollar. Fill them with gravel and they will stop bullets. Don't have any gravel? Get a truckload delivered to your safe spot today – if your place ever gets muddy, gravel can help you out with that as well. That pile of gravel could also make a nice place to store something that intruders will never find.

Get Your Health Sorted

If you have been putting off any elective surgery, it would be a good idea to use 2012 as your excuse to get it done. Laser surgery on your eyes should be considered if you have poor eyesight. Alternatively, buy a dozen of the cheapest spectacles you can find for your prescription, and store them at home, in your car, and at your survival spot.

2012 can also be used as an excuse to become fit and healthy. The first few days of a catastrophe could require you to perform physical tasks you are not accustomed to, so being prepared could make all the difference.

If you are reliant on medication due to poor diet or being overweight (particularly type 2 diabetes), now is the time to work on improving your health. Your medical supplies might not be available in the future.

If at all possible, stockpile your medications. Your doctor might be able to help you, either if you just tell them the truth, or if you say you are travelling to Africa for six months. In some online forums it has been suggested that antibiotics can be purchased from vets, but make sure you have researched this thoroughly (for the specific thing you are stockpiling) before trusting such advice...

Communications

Most people will struggle to just achieve their safe spot and a stockpile of supplies. While I have daydreamt about setting up a 2012 shortwave / ham radio broadcast, I accept that I don't have the time to learn and setup a suitable system. Hopefully there will be post-SHTF broadcasters for us to tune in to, and therefore make sure you have a good radio and means of local two-way communication.

Freeplay make good quality survival radios, solar or hand-cranked (mine has both), that receive all the bands including shortwave. Be wary of the cheapest options, the quality can be so low that they are unusable. I've had hand-cranks that have snapped upon first use, and solar radios that fail to charge. So at the very least, get them out of the box and use them, so that you can trust they will work later. All-in-one gadgets that include sirens and torches are appealing, but you are better off buying individual quality gadgets, even if that means they take up more space.

Walkie-talkies can be found reasonably cheap, and they are fun to test. Make sure you have a set or three. I guarantee you will use them if/when cell phones cease to function. If you are concerned that you might be overheard, buy a pair of military surplus field telephones for your survival retreat. And learn how to use them. Another solution is owning a marine band radio – not many people will be monitoring those bands miles inland.

Consider a multi-band police scanner:

- Be the first to hear about a local catastrophe
- Stay informed about crimes during an emergency
- Keep safe from the police if you decide you need to loot... or any other survival activity that a by-the-rules police officer might disapprove of. The last place you want to be is behind bars as that tsunami approaches

EMP Attack

An electromagnetic pulse basically fries electronics. Nuclear bombs are also EMPs, and terrorists could set-off a purpose-built EMP device – if you live near government facilities, or say Wall Street, or a Google data centre, be mindful of this possibility.

The following is from a 2004 report to US Congress titled *Report of the Commission to Assess the Threat to the United States from Electromagnetic Pulse (EMP) Attack*:

Several potential adversaries have or can acquire the capability to attack the United States with a high-altitude nuclear weapon-generated electromagnetic pulse (EMP). A determined adversary can achieve an EMP attack capability without having a high level of sophistication.

EMP is one of a small number of threats that can hold our society at risk of catastrophic consequences. EMP will cover the wide geographic region within line of sight to the nuclear weapon. It has the capability to produce significant damage to critical infrastructures and thus to the very fabric of US society, as well as to the ability of the United States and Western nations to project influence and military power.
http://www.empcommission.org/docs/empc_exec_rpt.pdf

A best-selling novel on this scenario from 2009 is *One Second Later*, read the plot summary here:
http://en.wikipedia.org/wiki/One_Second_After
(it also has a forward by 2012 presidential candidate Newt Gingrich).

Antique tube radios, for example the Zenith H-500 shortwave radio, are safe from EMPs.

Modern cars have electronic parts that will be fried by an EMP. So, in this regard, the older your vehicle is (as long as it is dependable), the better. In the USA, cars and trucks have had electronic ignitions since the mid to late 70s. If that's the only electronic part in your vehicle, keeping a spare in a Faraday Cage enables you to quickly get your vehicle functioning.

Given that a pre-1975 car should be quite cheap (if you can find a reliable car that old...), perhaps have one at home as well as your every-day modern car. And if you can afford it, have one at your safe spot as well. If they are the same make/model, you can use one for spare parts.

Speaking of vehicles at your safe spot, strongly consider purchasing an old diesel tractor. I guarantee you will find uses for it, SHTF or not.

Faraday Cage

This is a box or room that provides magnetic shielding. In the crudest sense, it is a metal box with a non-metal lining. It's a good place to store spare electronic items, such as car components, a screen device (like an iPod touch or iPad), cell phone, radio or camera.

I have not built one myself (yet) and I have searched in vain for a cheap retail product. Your only options are to build one yourself or buy an expensive industrial one. Homemade cages can be tested by seeing if a wireless device gets reception inside.

Instructions on how to build a proper Faraday cage yourself are here:
http://www.jeddaniels.com/2007/faraday-cage-part-1/
http://www.faradaycage.org/

The main difference in quality between those above and those below is having it grounded.

Making an el-cheapo version yourself:
http://suburbansurvivalblog.com/budget-faraday-cage-for-small-electronics
http://www.schoolofpreparation.com/2011/06/faraday-cage-on-a-budget/
http://www.survival-preps.com/index.php?topic=1642.0

ZipperTubing have components:
http://www.zippertubing.com/EMI-Shielding-Solutions.aspx

These companies will build one for you:
http://www.herzan.com/products/electromagnetic-interference-isolation/faraday-cages.html
http://www.faradaycages.com/index2.php?p=Content&id=132&nav=Faraday%20cages&nav_grp=Prefabricated%20faraday%20cage

Staying at Home (instead of having a safe spot)

James Wesley Rawles makes an important point in *How To Survive The End Of The World As We Know It* – your homes are **not** very secure. Modern homes typically have:

- Large glass windows without bars or shutters
- Easy access for vehicles
- Parent's rooms sometimes not alongside children's rooms
- Windows next to, or in, exterior doors
- Sliding glass doors

Our homes are so easy to break in to, that many of us rely on electronic products to secure our homes. After the SHTF they might not work, and the police & security services we depend on might not be available.

Post-SHTF Trading and Bartering

Most people will be focusing on the primary objectives of food, water, safety and general survival. But when everything has settled down, the post-SHTF environment might be one without a cash currency. Suddenly, de facto currencies will emerge, and lots of useful items will be pivotal when people trade. Having skills and knowledge in these areas could give you great advantages for on-going survival.

Anything that will be valuable after a disaster, but is cheap now, could be hoarded by you.

Coins. I read an article recently about one of the few individuals who made billions from predicting and betting on the Global Financial Crisis. His next step was to bet on countries defaulting on debts, but as a personal sideline, he had just bought a million dollars worth of nickels. His reasoning – the metal in a nickel is worth more than 6c. Post-SHTF paper notes might be used as toilet paper, but metal will still be valuable, so coins could continue as a currency.

Equipment. If you think back to gold rush days, those who made the most money (aside from the very lucky miner) where selling shovels, selling whiskey, or they had a set of scales. Post-SHTF you could be the person with the scales, or

- In the USA, use-by dates on canned goods are cryptic – have a Julian calendar and mealtime.org chart printed out.
- A voltmeter can quickly tell you if a battery is any good.
- For gold, you'll need equipment like an acid-test kit, touchstone and test needles – as well as a scale.

Beggars

Not often discussed is the possibility that regular, non-violent folk might turn up at your safe spot and seek charity. Before this happens, your group needs to work out a policy on this. Even if you think it can be decided on a case-by-case basis, you still need to prepare.

They could be elderly, or they could have children, or have other qualities that make you more inclined to help.

The best solution is to deal with these people away from your retreat, intercept them before they know where your safe spot is. Ideally some kind of road block, if you have enough people to keep one manned. But you need to make up a reason for why they cannot travel further down the road, a reason other than "because that's where we live". It could be a chemical leak, shootouts between X and Y, disease or even escaped zoo animals – whatever suits your culture and surroundings. Would you visit a property if they have a hand-scrawled sign that says "Please don't come any closer, we have Ebola"?

Alternatively, pretend to be one of them. Squat in an abandoned house, up the road from where your group really is. Look like you are barely surviving, with minimal supplies and comforts. When you intercept the visitors, you can assess them there and then. If you decide to help them, supplies can be brought down, and then can be asked to head off in a different direction. Or you can convince them that you went to the end of that road and have already scavenged all there was.

Another option is to confront them remotely. At the boundaries of your safe spot, have signs that straight-out say "We are armed to the teeth, and we are mean, and if you enter this property we will shoot you dead". Preferably position them so that only those who are certain to be visiting you will see them, and not someone just driving by.

If possible, have a loudspeaker system. A booming voice saying "Back off or we will shoot" is much more effective than meeting them physically, especially because they can't argue back.

Unexpected visitors could also be seeking medical help. If you have somewhere other than your main residence, that is where you should put them. And be very wary of any disease that they may be carrying.

Natural Defences

Natural obstacles that restrict access to your retreat can be very effective. As long as they look natural, all a visitor is going to think is "that way is too difficult". Whether they approach by vehicle or foot, any of the following could be sufficient:

- River, mud, swamp
- Thorny bushes
- Jungle or thick bush
- Scree
- Hedgerow
- A bull
- Geese (many people are scared of them, and they are good at sounding the alarm)

Further Reading

I highly recommend that you purchase the following books. They will provide you with all the information you need, from trustworthy authors who go into a greater detail on many of the topics I have touched upon. For example, the first four books combined have 128 pages on the topic of water.

How To Survive the End of the World As We Know It - James Wesley, Rawles

When All Hell Breaks Loose – Cody Lundin

When Technology Fails – Matthew Stein (get the latest edition)

Dare To Prepare – Holly Drennan Deyo (get the latest edition)

Where There Is No Dentist – Murray Dickson
Where There Is No Doctor – Gerard S. Doyle

Appendix 1 – Solar Storms

Solar Storms in a Nutshell

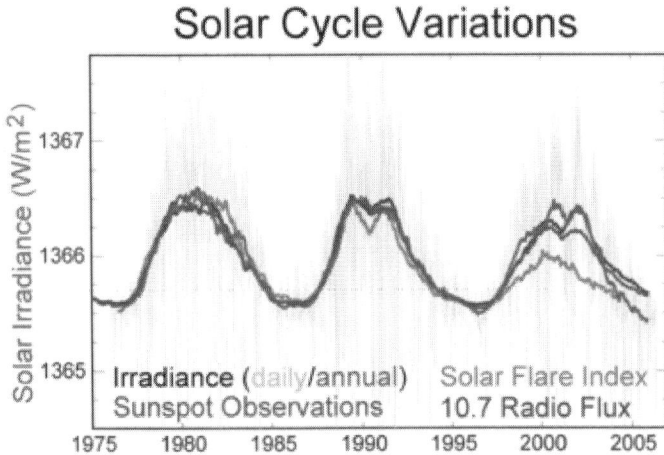

Solar Cycle Variations

[Source: Wikipedia]

Our Sun has a cycle of roughly 11 years. At the maximum/peak there are many more sunspots than at the minimum, and 50 times as many solar flares. The next maximum is due in late 2012 / early 2013.

Solar flares are sometimes accompanied by solar proton events and coronal mass ejections (see below). CMEs that are directed towards Earth can interact with our planet's magnetic field to produce a geomagnetic storm. Not every solar storm will produce all three elements but the largest solar storms typically do.

The Components of a Solar Storm

Solar Flares

Arrival Time: 8 minutes (speed of light)

Effect Duration: 1-2 hours

Harm: Electromagnetic radiation in the form of X-rays, extreme ultraviolet rays, gamma ray radiation and radio bursts. They can disrupt radar, satellite communications and radio.

Solar Proton Event

Arrival Time: 15 minutes to a few hours

Effect Duration: Days

Harm: Cosmic Rays which can cause satellite disorientation, spacecraft electronics damage, spacecraft solar panel degradation, extreme radiation hazard to astronauts, high altitude aircraft radiation, shortwave radio fades and disruption in polar regions, ozone layer depletion, cardiac arrest, dementia and cancer.

Coronal Mass Ejection

Arrival time: 2 or 4 days

Effect Duration: Days

Harm: CMEs consist of gas and charged plasma of energy particles A flood of charged particle and electrons in the ionosphere flow from west to east, inducing powerful electrical currents in the ground that surge through natural rock. CMEs can have the following affects: radar errors, radio anomalies, compass errors, electrical power blackouts, oil and gas pipeline corrosion, phone line & equipment damage, electrical shock hazard, electrical fires, heart attacks and strokes. CMEs are also the cause of auroras.

Source: http://www.breadandbutterscience.com/SSTA.pdf

Here are a few examples of modern harm from solar storms, followed by the most famous storm to date. More details can be found at http://www.solarstorms.org/SRefStorms.html

1921 - Telegraph system down west of the Mississippi, Central New England railroad station destroyed by fire

1942 - Allied radar disrupted during WW2

1972 - Transformer explodes in British Columbia

1984 - Air Force One loses communications en route to China

1989 - Quebec power outage

1989 - Toronto stock exchange computers crash

1994 - Canada's Anik E1 satellite goes off air for 7 hours, affecting news and telephone services. Then Anik E2 goes off air for good

2011 - On Valentine's Day some radio communications were lost, causing some polar flights to be re-routed

September 1, 1859 - The Carrington Event

Just before noon... English astronomer Richard C. Carrington was sketching a curious group of sunspots—curious on account of the dark areas' enormous size. At 11:18 a.m. he witnessed an intense white light flash from two locations within the sunspot group. He called out in vain to anyone in the observatory to come see the brief five-minute spectacle, but solitary astronomers seldom have an audience to share their excitement. Seventeen hours later in the Americas a second wave of auroras turned night to day as far south as Panama. People could read the newspaper by their crimson and green light. Gold miners in the Rocky Mountains woke up and ate breakfast at 1 a.m., thinking the sun had risen on a cloudy day. Telegraph systems became unusable across Europe and North America.

From *Scientific American, Aug 2008*
http://www.scientificamerican.com/article.cfm?id=bracing-for-a-solar-superstorm

In New York thousands of people lined the streets to view the auroral display, which was seen across North America:

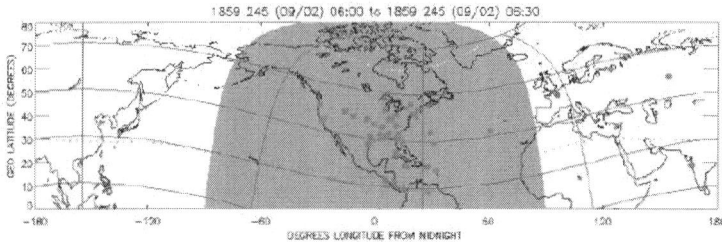

1859 245 (09/02) 06:00 to 1859 245 (09/02) 06:30

From August 28 through September 4, auroral displays of extraordinary brilliance were observed throughout North and South America, Europe, Asia, and Australia, and were seen as far south as Hawaii, the Caribbean, and Central America in the Northern Hemisphere and in the Southern Hemisphere as far north as Santiago, Chile.

from **Severe Space Weather Events**
https://download.nap.edu/catalog.php?record_id=12507

Remarkably, in some U.S. telegraph offices, operators disconnected the batteries and sent telegraphs *using only the current induced by the aurora*. But then life went on as usual and the Carrington Event was soon forgotten about. Even for scientists it was a curiosity, about as important as studying the seventh wave at the seashore... and it is only recently that this curiosity has been considered a serious threat to our lives.

The Sun Can Harm Our Infrastructure

Since 1859 we have seen the arrival of electronics, and with time our reliance on electronics has grown exponentially. A massive solar storm can harm our electrical grids, without which electronic products cannot operate (unless they run on batteries). Apart from some relatively minor events, the Sun has not yet attacked our grids, but that could just be good luck. In a primary sense, a repeat of the Carrington Event would most likely cause the following damage:

Power Grids - in March 1989 an X15 flare caused the entire Hydro Quebec system to blackout, with 6 million customers going without electricity for between 9 hours and several days. During the last solar maximum of 2000/2001, NASA estimates that the wholesale cost of electricity in the USA rose by $500 million to cover the costs of solar storm damage.

Railway Tracks - the tracks are long metal conductors. Currents from a CME can damage signaling systems and ignite fires in railroad control stations.

Oil and Gas Pipelines - can suffer from corrosion and potentially failure.

Telephone Land Lines and Undersea Cables - like railway tracks and pipelines, phone lines and cables are also conductors. The induced current (from a CME) can damage transmission lines and any attached equipment tied to those lines. It can also cause equipment fires and people could receive severe electrical shocks.

Satellites - as an example, Japan's Advanced Satellite for Cosmology and Astrophysics stopped functioning due to a solar storm in July 2000, and due to power losses it crashed to Earth eight months later. A bigger storm will likely knock out more satellites, including those that provide communications and GPS.

Radio and GPS - an X17 flare in Oct 2003 disrupted GPS functionality. According to the US Navy's report, (http://www.nrl.navy.mil/content_images/05FA5.pdf) "the FAA's Wide Area Augmentation System (WAAS), which uses GPS for aircraft navigation, was seriously impacted during the severe storms on October 29 and 30, and resulted in commercial aircraft being unable to use the WAAS for precision approaches."

But the flow on effect would be substantial. Homeland Security created this graphic that is really just a brief overview of how inter-connected these things are:

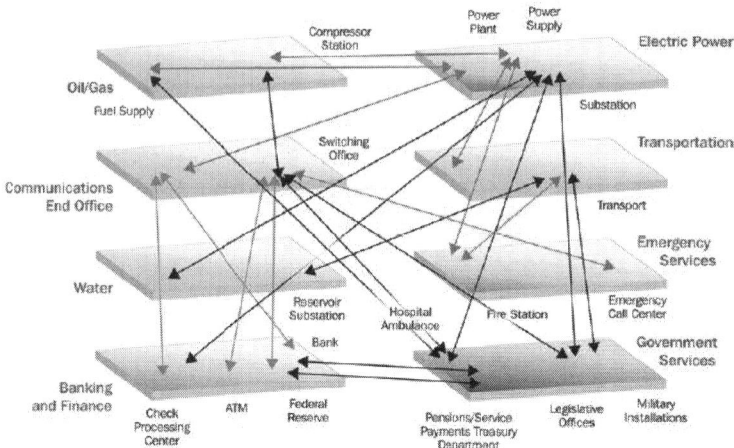

Here are just some of things we'd need to live without:

Infrastructure - banks won't be able to operate, nor will ATMs - they also use GPS for time stamping transactions. Traffic lights won't work, causing traffic jams initially. Police and emergency services will struggle to communicate. Empty store shelves will not be refilled. Almost everyone will be unable to work their regular job.

Water - some cities have gravity-fed water available, but in most places we rely on electrical pumps to get water to our homes. Electricity is also needed at water purification plants. Apart from drinking water, consider that we use it to wash, to flush toilets, and to move sewage away from our homes. Without electricity many sewage plants will not operate normally.

Heating and Cooling - the loss of these could kill people during the winter and summer months.

Energy and Fuel - pipelines can fail, and the normal way to access stored fuel is with an electric pump. While manual pumping might get gasoline out at a gas station, the authorities or thugs will likely be in control.

And then there's a special danger:

Nuclear Power Plants - without electricity there's only diesel generators to keep the plant cool and avoid meltdown. It would not be surprising if the amount of diesel on hand is low, and the ability to obtain more or even ask for more could be low in a dark USA.

Put all the above together and you invoke the butterfly effect... one example is that crime will increase, due to looting. To keep the peace, looters would need to be arrested and jailed. But to operate jails with no electricity becomes problematic - no video surveillance, difficulties in providing food and water and so on - which means a lot more police need to be deputized, removing able-bodied men from other useful tasks. A police chief might decide that looting is a hanging offence...

Why Are Power Grids Vulnerable?

Transformer Damage

Scientific American explains it well:

Large transformers are electrically grounded to Earth and thus susceptible to damage caused by geomagnetically induced direct current (DC). The DC flows up the transformer ground wires and can lead to temperature spikes of 200 degrees Celsius or higher in the transformer windings, causing coolant to vaporize and **literally frying the transformer**. Even if transformers avoid this fate, the induced current can cause their magnetic cores to saturate during one half of the alternating-current power cycle, distorting the 50- or 60-hertz waveforms. Some of the power is diverted to frequencies that electrical equipment cannot filter out. Instead of humming at a pure pitch, transformers would begin to chatter and screech. Because a magnetic storm affects transformers all over the country, the condition can rapidly escalate to a network-wide collapse of voltage regulation.

Grids operate so close to the margin of failure that it would not take much to push them over. According to studies by John G. Kappenman of Metatech Corporation, the magnetic storm of May 15, 1921, would have caused a blackout affecting half of North America had it happened today. **A much larger storm, like that of 1859, could bring down the entire grid.** Other industrial countries are also vulnerable, but North America faces greater danger because ofits proximity to the north magnetic pole. Because of the physical damage to transformers, full recovery and replacement of damaged components might take weeks or even months. Kappenman testified to Congress in 2003 that "the ability to provide meaningful emergency aid and response to an impacted population that may be in excess of 100 million people will be a difficult challenge."

The U.S. Congress has voted against providing funding that would harden the power grid and eliminate the possibility of a massive failure. It could be the worst decision they ever made. Other power grids that are reasonably close to the poles, such as Europe, Russia, Australia, Argentina and South Africa are also at risk.

What Are The Odds?

Scientists guesstimate that a solar storm with the magnitude of the Carrington Event will only happen once every 500 years (based on nitrates found in ice cores representing the last 450 years). Storms with half its intensity should hit every 50 years or so. The last one occurred on November 13, 1960, and led to global geomagnetic disturbances and radio outages. The next is due now, at a time when satellites are substantially more important, and power grids are more vulnerable. Larger storms than the Carrington Event will also happen, although we don't know how frequently. One model (http://www.breadandbutterscience.com/SSTA.pdf) has shown that a storm 1000 times as strong is possible.

Heart Attacks and Strokes

Amazingly, studies have shown that during solar storms the frequency of hospital admissions for heart attacks and strokes is roughly double that of quiet solar periods. Magnetic pulses are thought to be the cause. Geomagnetic storms have also been linked to depression, enhanced anxiety, sleep disturbances, altered moods and psychiatric admissions (up 36%). Presumably there would be far greater increases during a storm like the Carrington Event.

Are We Prepared?

NOAA's Space Weather Prediction Center provides daily space weather reports (their data appears at SpaceWeather.com) to businesses and government agencies. Its annual budget is a mere $6 million. It does provide advance warnings so that businesses can take precautionary measures, but there is a great deal of variability between their predictions and the actual damage that can occur. And with a Carrington-type event, the warning provides a mere 10-minute window in which to act.

When warning us about incoming geomagnetic storms, the NOAA's only source of data is the Advanced Composition Explorer (ACE) satellite. It was launched in 1997, and according the the U.S. National Academy of Sciences in 2009, it is "well beyond its planned operational life". I take this to mean it could fail any time, and there is no backup satellite! And all current safety measures become redundant - we won't be able to remove vulnerable equipment from the grid before it is too late. "ACE is a single point of failure and it's old," said William Murtagh, program coordinator for NOAA's Space Weather Prediction Center. "Every time I have a space weather storm I cringe a little bit that our very own space weather satellite doesn't succumb to the storms I'm relying on it to help forecast."

Power grids are prepared to some degree. The Hydro Quebec blackout of 1989 was due to circuit breakers shutting down the system before the flare could fry transformers. It is not known how dependable such safety systems are, for they have not been sufficiently put to the test.

And of course human error is easily possible. The decision of when and how to shut down an electrical system might come down to one or two individuals. They might delay the shut-down too long, or they might think their jobs were at risk if they mistakenly switched off power to entire cities. The devastating Queensland floods of 2011 were the result of a similar type of human error - and they had days to make their decisions, not ten minutes.

Several million Preppers are prepared for this and various other catastrophes. That leaves hundreds of millions of Americans who are not prepared, as well as governments and infrastructures that have not made provisions for long-term losses of electricity.

Official Vulnerability Estimate

The following (long) quote is from *Severe Space Weather Events*, a report commissioned by the National Research Council.

Severe space weather has the potential to pose serious threats to the future North American electric power grid. Recently, Metatech Corporation carried out a study under the auspices of the Electromagnetic Pulse Commission and also for the Federal Emergency Management Agency (FEMA) to examine the potential impacts of severe geomagnetic storm events on the U.S. electric power grid. These assessments indicate that severe geomagnetic storms pose a risk for long-term outages to major portions of the North American grid.

John Kappenman remarked that the analysis shows "not only the potential for large-scale blackouts but, more troubling, . . . the potential for permanent damage that could lead to extraordinarily long restoration times."

While a severe storm is a low-frequency-of-occurrence event, it has the potential for long-duration catastrophic impacts to the power grid and its users. Impacts would be felt on interdependent infrastructures, with, for example, potable water distribution affected within several hours; perishable foods and medications lost in about 12-24 hours; and immediate or eventual loss of heating/air conditioning, sewage disposal, phone service, transportation, fuel resupply, and so on. Kappenman stated that the effects on these interdependent infrastructures could persist for multiple years, with a potential for significant societal impacts and with economic costs that could be measurable in the several-trillion dollars-per-year range.

...The least understood aspect of this threat is the permanent damage to power grid assets and how that will impede the restoration process. Transformer damage is the most likely outcome, although other key assets on the grid are also at risk. In particular, transformers experience excessive levels of internal heating brought on by stray flux when GICs cause a transformer's magnetic core to saturate and to spill flux outside the normal core steel magnetic circuit. Kappenman stated that previous well-documented cases have involved heating failures that caused melting and burn-through of large-amperage copper windings and leads in these transformers. These multi-ton apparatus generally cannot be repaired in the field, and if damaged in this manner, they need to be replaced with new units, which have manufacture lead times of 12 months or more.

...In summary, present U.S. grid operational procedures are based largely on limited experience, generally do not reduce GIC flows, and are unlikely to be adequate for historically large disturbance events. Historically large storms have a potential to cause power grid blackouts and transformer damage of unprecedented proportions, long-term blackouts, and lengthy restoration times, and chronic shortages for multiple years are possible. As Kappenman summed up, "An event that could incapacitate the network for a long time could be one of the largest natural disasters that we could face."

Finally, I can recommend this Feb 2012 article from the IEEE, which concludes " *If we do nothing—if we stand by and wait for politicians to appreciate the risks and act on them—we may witness one of the worst catastrophes of all time* "

http://spectrum.ieee.org/energy/the-smarter-grid/a-perfect-storm-of-planetary-proportions/0

Solar Storm in 2012?

You don't need to be a scientist to know when a massive solar storm occurs – the auroras let everyone know. The auroras associated with the Carrington Event were seen worldwide, and at many low latitudes.

An ancient culture that lived at low latitudes (the Maya, for example) could have kept note of the rare instances when auroras were visible to them. This would be easy to achieve if they used a calendar like the Long Count calendar of the ancient Maya (and perhaps the Olmec before them).

Basic mathematical skills would be sufficient to notice a pattern in auroral appearances, and to predict the next. It is entirely possible that an ancient culture noticed a pattern in the biggest auroral displays, and predicted another for 2012.

If that is the case, the storm that is coming will far exceed in strength anything witnessed by modern scientists, and could even exceed anything they can imagine.

If not the Olmecs and their predecessors making the observations and prediction, there's a remote possibility that it was the ancient Egyptians. While there is no evidence for this, such ancient inter-continental contact would also help explain how the Maya and Aztec cultures learned how to build pyramids.

Appendix 2 – Asteroids and Comets

[The] story of how Phaëton, child of the sun, harnessed his father's chariot, but was unable to guide it along his father's course and so burnt up things on the earth and was himself destroyed by a thunderbolt, is a mythical version of the truth that there is at long intervals a variation in the course of the heavenly bodies and a consequent widespread destruction by fire of things on earth.

Plato
Timaeus

How Big Is The Risk?

Here is a rundown of the different sizes, their probabilities, the chances of us seeing them coming, and the theoretical approximates of the damage they could inflict. Because we know so little about the makeup of comets, I've lumped them in with asteroids for convenience.

1 kilometer diameter or larger
The aim of NASA and their various branches and allies is to discover at least 99% of these monsters.
http://neo.jpl.nasa.gov/faq/

A 10km asteroid strike would create waves in the Earth's crust higher than houses, and a blast of 500°C air travelling at 2500 kph. Any creature within 12 million sq km would be wiped out.(1) That's roughly the size of the USA, Europe or Australia

500 meter
According to Duncan Steel (2), we are unlikely to discover more than half of the asteroids and comets in our solar system with a 500 meter diameter. Just one of these would create a crater 10km wide, and destroy all life within 1,000sq km.(3)

100 meter
These are so small, in terms of our ability to discover them, that only a few percent are likely to be spotted, says Steel. If a 100m asteroid struck Earth at 19km/sec the resulting crater would be 2km across, and it would destroy all life within 200sq km. These hit Earth with an average frequency of one every 22,000 years.(4) Or according to Gerrit L. Verschuur, as often as every 1,000 years (5).

50 meter – Tunguska size
Objects with a diameter of 50-60 meters pass closer to Earth than the Moon about once per week.(6) Aside from the famous Tunguska incident, and serving as a reminder that Tunguska was not a "one-off", a smaller asteroid exploded mid-air over eastern Siberia in 1947, leaving "122 craters up to 26m wide and 5m deep."(7) It weighed about 70 tonnes.

They Strike Earth All The Time!

Meteors do make it to Earth – here are some examples that serve as a reminder:

1 meter – Barwell, UK – 1965
Roughly half of Coventry, a city of 300,000 that it passed over, say they heard it. Some of the high frequencies given off meant horses heard it before it became visible. Those that could see it through the evening clouds estimated the tail to be 20 degrees long. It broke up into many pieces, and although some struck buildings, nobody was hurt.

Astrophysicists from the Herzberg Institute in Ottawa, Canada, have estimated that an average of 16 buildings are damaged by meteorites each year, with a human being hit every nine years, sometimes fatally.(8)

Recorded deaths by meteorites and asteroids:

588 AD, 10 people, China

1490, supposedly 10,000 people, China

1511, Franciscan monk, Cremona, Italy

1650, Another monk (!), Milan, Italy

1647-54, 2 sailors at sea

1790, A farmer and cattle, France

1825 , A man, India

1827, A man, India

1874, Child, China

1879, Man in bed, Indiana, USA

1879, Farmer, France

1897, Horse, West Virginia, USA

1907, Entire family, China

1908, 2 people reported, Tunguska

1911, Dog, Egypt

1929, 1 member of a bridal party, Zvezvan, Yugoslavia

Buildings are stuck, and people nearly hit, most years. A recent example (**June 2009**) involved a German schoolboy, Gerrit Blank, who was left with a scar on his hand when he was grazed by a meteorite that left a 30cm-wide crater in the pavement.

In **1931**, three asteroid fragments struck a Brazilian jungle and 1,300 square kilometers of rainforest were destroyed by a wall of fire. (9)

On **February 1, 1994**, near the Marshall Islands in the western Pacific, a handful of fishermen witnessed a hundred-kiloton explosion (that's 10x Hiroshima) that momentarily flashed brighter than the sun. This asteroid has been estimated to be just 6-17 metres across, but plenty sufficient to decimate a city - so it was extremely fortunate (for humans) that it exploded above the ocean. According to Duncan Steel:

"It is therefore not surprising that the 10-meter-or-so asteroid that blew up over a largely vacant area of the western Pacific on February 1, 1994, producing an explosion equivalent to at least ten times that of the Hiroshima bomb (and possibly rather more), was not seen prior to impact. Surveillance satellites registered it as the brightest such explosion that they have picked up so far. Despite the efforts of numerous scientists in this area of study to make the military aware that such detonations do occur naturally, it appears that the U.S. President was awakened because the Pentagon thought that this incident might be a hostile nuclear explosion." (10)

Relatively Recent, Large Impacts

Merewether crater, west of Ungava Bay in Canada, is 200m in diameter and was formed less than 10,000 years ago. More recent is the Henbury crater cluster near Alice Springs, Australia. The twelve craters have been dated at between 2,000 and 6,000 years ago. The largest is 180m across and 15m deep. According to Aboriginal legend, the site is known as "sun walk fire devil rock", suggesting that the event had witnesses.

Recent Near Misses

In 1937 an asteroid called Hermes, with a diameter of one kilometer, became the closest recorded passage to Earth (since surpassed). When it crossed our orbit it was 780,000kms away, twice the distance of the moon. In terms of time, it missed us by a mere 5 hours. It was reported 2 months later, with newspapers claiming we almost witnessed the destruction of our planet. (11)

1989 – a 300m asteroid (known as 4581 Asclepius or 1989 FC) missed us by 690,000kms and 7 hours. It was not spotted until after it had flown by. It is due to return in 2012, but is not expected to come as close.
1991 – a 100m asteroid (1991 BA) passed within 170,000kms.
1996 – a 300–500 m asteroid, (1996 JA1_, passed within 450,000 km of Earth

In the near future, the number one concern is a 320 m asteroid known as 99942 Apophis. Although when first discovered it was considered to have a 1 in 17 chance of hitting Earth, it is now understood to only come as close as 25,600 kilometers – close enough to knock out a communications satellite!

What Are The Odds?

Given recent examples, it is easy to believe that incidences of humans being killed by such impacts are rare. However, when you consider the catastrophic impacts that happen less often (but when they do, can kill millions), the odds become a little bit more sobering. Austen Atkinson says the odds of being killed by a comet or asteroid is 1 in 24,000. (12) And then he points out that the odds of contracting mad-cow disease is 1 in 15 million, yet that scared most of the world enough to ban the importation of British beef.

1 in 24,000 is roughly the same odds for dying as a result of a plane crash. I'm not alone in worrying about this every time I board a plane...

The problem we have is easily understood – governments generally react after the fact, not before. It is only after some of us have suffered somehow that the government decides to do something about it – they are not in the business of scaring us with predictions of what might happen, unless it suits them (think pre-emptive military strikes).

The folk running the city of New Orleans were very aware of the risk of flooding they faced from hurricanes, and they chose to gamble that it wouldn't happen on their watch, a gamble that they lost with Katrina. Appropriate spending, relative to the risk they faced, would have saved New Orleans. If it is an "Act of God", our governments seem to universally elect to be underprepared for it. Especially when, in the case of New Orleans, to be prepared would have taken a commitment of $1 billion and 20 years.

At present, NASA's "Spaceguard Survey", which aims to spot Near-Earth Objects greater than 1 kilometer in diameter, has a budget of $4.1 million per year from 2006 through to 2012. This is a pitiful effort, relative to the risk, and explains why most new comets are discovered by amateurs.

Effect of a Comet/Asteroid Striking Earth

The easiest to predict is the most likely – the collision occurring in the ocean. First of all, here's some data regarding recent tsunamis caused by earthquakes and volcanoes...

1960: An earthquake in Chile with a magnitude of 9.5 (the largest magnitude ever recorded) caused the death of 6000 people worldwide. 61 of the victims were in Hawaii, as the result of a tsunami that arrived 14 hours later – when it struck it was 10-15 meters in height . The same tsunami killed 142 people in Japan, when it arrived 22 hours after the earthquake. By then its height had reduced to between 1 and 5 meters. The deep-water wave (the height of the tsunami before it reaches land) was only 20 cms.

2004: The Indian Ocean tsunami was caused by the second largest earthquake ever measured (9.1-9.3), and was much more devastating. It killed more than 225,000 people in eleven countries with waves as high as 30 meters. However, before reaching land it was mere 60 cms in height.

We don't know when an asteroid or meteor will strike Earth next, but we know that in the past there have been many – they leave a crater. The type of tsunami they can create has not been recorded by humans (as far as we know), so all we have are best guesses coming from experts.

The threat of tsunamis caused by asteroid impacts has only recently been recognized, due to the work of Jack Hills and Patrick Goda of the Los Alamos National Laboratory in New Mexico. They have performed calculations showing that the hypothetical 500-meter asteroid mentioned earlier would produce a deep water wave 50 to 100 meters in amplitude, even at a range of 1,000 kilometers from ground zero.

Since the tsunami height could be amplified by a factor of 20 or more in the run up as continental shelves are encountered, we are referring here to **a tsunami several kilometers in height.** Even if the impact were between New Zealand and Tahiti, the tsunami breaking on Japan would be perhaps 200 to 300 meters high, and heaven help New Zealand and Tahiti themselves!... (13)

In case you are wondering how far inland you would need to be to survive, formulas have been determined. A 200-300 meter tsunami hitting a populated coastline (buildings will slow it and hinder its advance) will travel 50-100 kilometers inland, or even further if the terrain is flat. (14)

If you are thinking to yourself "fair enough, but I can't imagine a tsunami that high ever occurring", consider this; coral has been found in Lanai, Hawaii, 326 meters above sea level, quite possibly due to a tsunami passing through.

There have been several studies made regarding the Tunguska event. Two figure it was an asteroid, with a diameter of 60, or 90-190 meters. Another study decided it was a comet with a diameter of 1200 meters. (15) According to Duncan Steel, generally speaking, anything that can make it through the atmosphere without disintegrating, and affect more than just the spot where it crashes, would need to be 50 meters wide (for an asteroid) and 100 meters wide (for a comet). To put it another way, if it hits the ocean we either won't notice, or there will be a substantial tsunami, and nothing in between. (16)

A 100-meter object will typically strike Earth once every 1,000 years, and if it struck land would lay waste to an area of about 10,000 square kilometers – roughly the same size as Connecticut. The deaths just from the impact would depend on the population density, but would be much less than if it struck the ocean. Shin Yabushita has calculated that the odds of most of the Pacific Rim cities being wiped out by an asteroid/comet driven tsunami, in the next century, is 1%. A sobering figure. (17)

In terms of survival, land and sea impacts are quite different. A sea impact will create a tsunami, and depending on the location, could wipe out many major cities. Once the waves subside, Earth is pretty much back to normal, but we will be missing the people and the infrastructure that were destroyed. While this would be tragic for the global economy, people living outside the path of the tsunami will still have their crops and climate, and life will go on. A terrestrial impact might cause less immediate damage, but create long-term hardships.

Overall, Gilmour and his colleagues have identified a dozen "environmental stresses" caused by the K-T impact. The strong winds and tsunamis lasted for a matter of hours; fires lasted for months, as did the darkness and cold partly caused by the fires; the greenhouse effect began to take grip as the darkness cleared, boosted early on by the presence of water vapour in the air, and maintained by the long-term presence of carbon dioxide; poisons and mutagens remained active for years, as did the effects of acid rain; the ozone layer must have been severely disrupted by the disturbance to the atmosphere, and then there was the volcanic activity triggered by the impact. (18)

As a recent example, the Gribbins mention a "relatively modest" forest fire in California, 1987, which reduced valley temperatures by 15 degrees Celsius for an entire week. With the ozone layer depleted by nitric oxides, crops would be burnt, and humans venturing outside unprotected would risk cancer. Few crops would survive acid rain, fires, extended periods of darkness and ozone depletion. Humans and animals would starve, and we would also miss the ability of plant life to remove carbon dioxide from our atmosphere. The amount of time it would take for Gaia to return to a steady state environment is not known.

The great K/T boundary extinction of 65 million years ago is a good example of how bad it can get, and how extinctions occur. A 15 kilometer wide asteroid crashed into North America. Debris from the impact was ejected into the atmosphere, and then fell as billions of tiny bullets. A fireball engulfed the continent, soot adding to the dust in the atmosphere. Global temperatures dropped by as much as 10 degrees Celsius. Plants died –they could not survive the triple-whammy of fire, acid rain and lack of sunlight. Large animals starved. Some smaller animals, those that didn't mind feeding on dead tissue and rotting vegetation, managed to survive, as a species. Phytoplankton, dependant on sunlight, died. Because it was the fundamental basis of the oceanic food chain, the oceans became more about death than life. It is estimated that 75 percent of all Earth's species became extinct following that singular asteroid impact.

Would we be warned? And how?

In March 1996, a declaration by the Council of Europe, discussing the dangers of Near-Earth Objects, and name-checking Tunguska and Shoemaker-Levy, said that the "possible consequences are so vast that every reasonable effort should be encouraged to minimize them." (19)

A single impact by a rock the size of the Millennium Dome could devastate the surface of the globe with an explosive release of energy five times more powerful than the entire world's nuclear arsenal. On 19 May 1996, just such an object came within 280,000 miles of Earth: six hours from collision.

Humankind could have been eradicated.

The asteroid (named JA1) sailed into our system - the largest object to approach Earth, other than the moon, since records began in 1833 - and was only four days away before two astronomers (Tim Spahr and Carl Hergenrother) in Tuscon, Arizona, detected it and alerted the US National Aeronautics and Space Administration (NASA).

No one was prepared. Nothing could be done to prevent its approach. Yet no one was told: no public warning was given. The world's powers watched the asteroid approach, impotent and unable to prevent the end of human civilization. At the last moment, when it was only 400,000 miles, or seven hours, away from impact, its trajectory carried it away from our world. (20)

A few months later physicist Edward Teller wrote to the British Prime Minister, warning him of the serious threat posed by asteroids and comets - Teller, as a key player in the development of the hydrogen bomb, knew all about how fragile human existence is. (21)

The same year the US Department of Defense created a report that said:

Due to a lack of awareness and emphasis, the world is not socially, economically or politically prepared to deal with the vulnerability of ...ECO (Earth Crossing Object) impacts and their potential consequences.

...These authors contend that the stakes are simply too high not to pursue direct and viable solutions to the ECO problem. Indeed, the survival of humanity is at stake. (22)

One of the brightest comets ever seen was Halle-Bopp. With a nucleus estimated at 40kms it is certainly large enough to wipe out all of humankind. It is rather discomforting to learn that we only noticed it in 1995, and if it happened to have been aimed straight at us, would have struck in 1997. Two years would not be enough time to plan/build/launch a defense.

While asteroids mostly follow the same plane of orbit as the planets, quite a narrow band of sky that is under regular observation – comets can come from anywhere, they can sneak up on us. Consequently comets tend to be discovered by amateur astronomers, while NASA lacks the funds (and perhaps willingness) to carry out full-sky observations.

It is not for me to speculate on our future ability to change the path of an asteroid or comet, should one have our planet in its sights. But based on what is currently known, it seems unlikely that we will be prepared to take on such an object if it was destined to crash into us in 2012. However, you never know what NASA might have been putting together in secret.

Therefore my presumption is this, we cannot thwart a comet or asteroid, and if one strikes us in 2012 there will be significant loss of life, depending on the size and location of impact. The bigger it is, the more likely we are to see it coming, yet the greater the odds of it wiping out all of humanity.

1. Peter Grego, *Collision Earth* (Blandford, 1998), 92.

2. Duncan Steel, *Rogue Asteroids and Doomsday Comets* (John Wiley & Sons, Inc., 1995), 222.

3. Grego, *Collision Earth*, 106.

4. Ibid.

5. Vershuur, Gerrit L., *Impact!: the threat of comets and asteroids*, 166

6. Steel, *Rogue Asteroids and Doomsday Comets*, 236.

7. Grego, *Collision Earth*, 79.

8. Ibid., 71.

9. Austen Atkinson, *Impact Earth* (Virgin, 1999), 81.

10. Steel, *Rogue Asteroids and Doomsday Comets*, 203-204.

11. Grego, *Collision Earth*, 101.

12. Atkinson, *Impact Earth*, 8.

13. Steel, *Rogue Asteroids and Doomsday Comets*, 40.

14. Ibid., 41.

15. "The Tunguska event," http://web.utk.edu/~comet/papers/nature/TUNGUSKA.html.

16. Steel, *Rogue Asteroids and Doomsday Comets*, 44.

17. Vershuur, Gerrit L., *Impact!: the threat of comets and asteroids*, 166.

18. John & Mary Gribbin, *Fire on Earth* (Pocket Books, 1996), 37.

19. Atkinson, *Impact Earth*, 84.

20. Ibid., 3.

21. Ibid., 4.

22. Ibid., 6.

Appendix 3 - Dark Comet in 2012?

> When beggars die there are no comets seen. The heavens themselves blaze forth the death of princes.
> **Shakespeare**
> *Julius Caesar*

When considering what might cause us grief in 2012, few if any researchers consider the start of the Mayan Long Count calendar to have any importance. This is surprising, because the reason for the calendar beginning on August 11 3114BC might contain clues about 2012 itself. After all, the Mayan culture did not exist 5,000 years ago, so either they randomly chose an ancient date on a whim, or an earlier civilization was behind the calendar, and they knew something important occurred on that date.

What could happen in 3114BC, and also in 2012AD? No civilization has lasted that long, so they are unlikely to be man-made events. Any natural events that occur so infrequently on Earth are virtually impossible to predict (volcanic eruptions for example). So that leaves us with astronomical events.

The astrology of the pair of dates has been well studied, so we can rule out alignments of the stars and planets. That leaves the Sun, which we barely understand today, and comets. Is there a comet with a periodicy of 5000 years, due to return in 2012? Without any evidence from 3114BC it is impossible to say. Given that we are now near the end of the Mayan 5th age, could their calendar be designed to cover five orbits of a comet? And end catastrophically in 2012?

Most people have not heard of Comet Caesar (it didn't even have a Wikipedia entry at the time of writing), and hopefully this will remain so. However, if we are to suffer a terrible tragedy in 2012, it is currently my leading candidate, and the purpose of this article is to explain why.

Comet Caesar

Comet Caesar was the most famous comet of its day, and one of the brightest ever witnessed. It was visible during an annual Roman festival held in 44BC, shortly after Julius Caesar's death. The following quotes are from *The Greatest Comets in History: Broom Stars and Celestial Scimitars* by David Seargent:

This was the comet that blazed in the skies of Rome following the assassination of Julius Caesar and which became immortalized by the Romans on the reverse of a coin bearing a portrait of Augustus struck in honor of the great Julius.

...According to Pliny, Octavian wrote that "On the very days of my games, a comet was visible over the course of seven days, in the northern region of the heavens. It rose at about the eleventh hour of the day and was bright and plainly seen from all lands".

...In the fourth century of our era, Servius presented an account that had the comet visible for 3 days and visible at midday and during the daytime.

Comet Caesar is a *parabolic comet* - a comet that returns less frequently than every 200 years. Most parabolic comets have orbits significantly longer than 200 years, and very few have ever been observed to make a complete orbit.[1] Astronomers expect 50 percent of parabolic comets will receive gravitational nudges that cause them to never orbit the Sun again. Those that remain in orbit should be slowed with each passage, eventually becoming intermediate or short-period comets.[2] Therefore we either never see them again, or they take so long to return that we don't know which, if any, have historical records they match up with.

In my search for the most likely 2012 culprit, I have constantly asked myself, could the ancients have predicted this? Asteroids and comets are definitely predictable in a broad sense, and all that it takes is observation and mathematics. Such calculations are not easy. They require recalculating the orbit for every day of every year, according to where the object is then located, and how the planets are affecting its course. If ancient astronomers had considered the period of a comet or asteroid to be fixed, rather than varying due to the gravitational influences of planets, then there may have been inaccuracies in any 2012 prediction they made. However the daily recalculations were certainly not impossible in ancient times.

Predictability of Comets

Perhaps the most famous comet, even today, is Halley's Comet. Edmond Halley - as well as a team of French mathematicians - predicted the return of this comet, not just from knowing the dates of its past visits, but by calculating the gravitational effects of planets like Saturn and Jupiter. *They did this by hand.*

A single line in the Talmud suggests that 1st century Jewish astronomers were also aware of the periodicy of Halley's Comet:

"a star which appears once in seventy years that makes the captains of the ships err".

To go from calculating the return of a comet, to having knowledge that it will probably strike Earth, is a major leap. Although that is not to say they weren't merely predicting the return of a spectacular comet, let's investigate the possibility that an ancient culture was capable of predicting the actual impact of a comet in 2012.
First of all, for this hypothesis to have any validity, the comet must be a long period one; that is, it must pass our planet less frequently than once every 200 years. More frequent comets would be well known by modern astronomers, and would most likely have their future orbits determined.

According to Wikipedia, there are just 40 known comets with a periodicy greater than 200 years (or non-periodic comets). Of these, 38 have been observed since 1577AD. The only prior dates were 1106AD and 44BC. To me this suggests that a great many earlier observations would have been made, we just don't have evidence of such. The Great Comet of 1106AD was seen from Europe to Japan. A Welsh text said of it:

In that year there was seen a star wonderful to behold, throwing out behind it a beam of light of the thickness of a pillar in size and of exceeding brightness.
http://en.wikipedia.org/wiki/X/1106_C1

Were we to have detailed records of comets from more historical times, we might have a similar description with which we could determine the periodicy of the 1106 comet. Without this, we have nothing to base its return on - could be tomorrow, could be never. [3]

You could say the same about Comet Caesar, the aforementioned earliest recorded comet of 44BC. Without another record of it, we cannot determine when it will return next. While there may not be any surviving record of a prior passage, perhaps we can make an implication from the Long Count calendar. If the end of the calendar is actually the date a comet will strike Earth, what is the most logical reason for the start date?

If, and this is obviously pure speculation, it had been observed in 3114BC, and again in 44BC, could it be returning once again in 2012? With a precise periodicy of 1025.2 years (which equals four Mayan Short Counts) we get the following sequence of dates:

3114BC - start of the Long Count calendar

2089BC - 2104/2105 is when the Great Flood occurred according to the Hebrew Calendar

1064BC - 1077 was the end of the Egyptian New Kingdom, marking the beginning of Egypt's decline

39BC - Comet Caesar was witnessed in 44BC

987AD - Dark Ages

2012AD - end of the Long Count calendar

Is 39BC close enough to 44BC? In 1758 the French astronomers who calculated the return of Halley's Comet determined that the gravitational effects of Saturn and Jupiter would make a difference of 618 days to its existing orbit, or almost 2 years. Is a difference of 5 years within 5 orbits outside the realms of possibility?

Variable Periodicy of Comets

When Comet Hyakutake was discovered in 1996, astronomers determined that on the way in to our solar system it had an estimated periodicy of 17,000 years, yet after having its orbit disturbed by the largest planets, its new course meant it would take between 72,000 and 114,000 years to return.

When 23P/Brorsen-Metcalf was first discovered it was closest to Earth in August 1847. After completing its orbit it was back in that approximate spot in October 1919, and again in August 1989. The two observed periods were 72 years and 70 years. That's roughly a 3% deviation between 2 orbits.

The periodicy of a comet can vary from a little, to a lot, to so much we never see it again. It is entirely possible that Comet Caesar was seen the very same years as the Great Flood, the end of the Egyptian New Kingdom, the start of the Long Count calendar - and will return in 2012.

Where are the records?

…they were either not observed or were observed and recovered by illiterate, uneducated peasants. It was quite unthinkable that the sophisticated urban theologian of A.D. 1000… should take seriously the allegations of such rabble that stones fell from the sky.

…Modern astronomers seeking accounts of ancient astronomical events …find the records of medieval Europe sparse at best.[4]

To explain the absence of records for Comet Caesar prior to 44BC is easy – lost in the annals of history that never made it. But what of 987AD? Could it really go from observed in 44BC, to not observed at all? Or has the record from 987AD +/-3 years, just disappeared?

The former possibility is covered by the concept of dark comets, described below. To answer the latter possibility, 987 was in the Dark Ages, renowned for a lack of records. In fact so lacking that some researchers have speculated that the era never existed at all!

Halley's Comet was observed in 837 according to records from Japan, China, and Germany. The next observation was in 912, and was recorded in the Annals of Ulster, like this: "A dark and rainy year. A comet appeared". There is no specific record of its return in 990, and was next spotted in 1066, where it was recorded as having an influence on the Battle of Hastings.

The only mention of a comet circa 987AD (when I approximately hypothesize Comet Caesar would have returned) is indirect, and attributed to Eilmer of Malmesbury, a Benedictine monk:
You've come, have you? - You've come, you source of tears to many mothers. It is long since I saw you; but as I see you now you are much more terrible, for I see you brandishing the downfall of my country
http://en.wikipedia.org/wiki/Eilmer_of_Malmesbury

He described this appearance in 1066. Because the previous passage of Halley's Comet would have been in 990AD, and he was an "old man" in 1066, it is believed that he could have seen the comet when he was 5 years old, and have would been 76 years old in 1066 when he was quoted. But what if he was just a few years older in 1066, and was actually recalling a comet he witnessed in 987AD? Could he have seen the most recent passing of Comet Caesar, and not Halley's Comet, in the closing years of the tenth century?

Taking a different angle, if there is no specific record of Halley's Comet in 990AD, it fits that a return of Comet Caesar circa 987AD also avoided any record that survives to this day.

For some, a simple lack of record will suffice, and the hypothesis is feasible. For the others, I will describe a mechanism from which the comet rapidly loses visibility.

Dark Comets

There's only one difference between dark comets and regular comets - we won't see the approach of the dark comet.

In early 2009 many news articles reported the findings of British astronomers Bill Napier (Cardiff University) and David Asher (Armagh Observatory), and reading them sent a shiver down my spine, prompting me to research the possibilities further.

"There is a case to be made that dark, dormant comets are a significant but largely unseen hazard," says Napier.

...periodic comet showers appear to correlate with the dates of ancient impact craters found on Earth, which would suggest that most impactors in the past were comets, not asteroids.

Now Napier and Asher warn that some of these comets may still be zipping around the solar system. Other observations support their case. The rate that bright comets enter the solar system implies there should be around 3000 of them buzzing around, and yet only 25 are known.[5]

Until now it was commonly accepted that more than 90% of meteors and comets that could cause us harm were known and tracked by astronomers and government agencies. That thousands of comets that are potentially heading straight for us are not known or tracked is rather frightening. How can a comet become dark?

The science is actually quite easy to understand. Comets start out with ice on their surface. Every time they orbit around the Sun, the heat melts some ice. Eventually there is no ice left. And the only way we can easily see comets is from light reflecting off the ice.

In 1983, Comet IRAS-Araki-Alcock passed by Earth at a distance of 5 million kilometres, the closest known pass by any known comet for 200 years. It was spotted only two weeks ahead of its closest approach. "It had only 1 per cent of its surface active," says Napier. Comet Borrelly, visited by NASA's Deep Space 1 probe in 2001, was found to have extremely dark patches over much of its surface.[6]

Clark Chapman, from the Southwest Research Institute in Boulder, Colorado, is not so concerned, saying that the dark comets 'would absorb sunlight very well' and therefore should be possible to detect from the heat they would emit.

I'm not qualified to judge this statement, but from a layman's point of view, I would think a hand-held mirror reflecting the sun's light from a mile away is far more easily seen than a slab of rock that is so hot you could fry an egg on it.

Here are a couple of examples of lost comets. One of the reasons they are no longer observed could be that they have lost their luminosity.

18D/Perrine-Mrkos - seen in 1896 and 1909, then 1955, then 1969, and not since.

5D/Brorsen - first spotted in 1846, last seen in 1879. With an orbital period of 5.5 years. Has been as close as 0.52 AU to Earth, and as far as 1.5AU. Japanese astronomers hoped to spot it in 1976, but failed.

The orbital period of 5D/Brorsen suggests it could be passing by in 2012, if it is still on course. There is even a possible case of a dark comet harming us (in a roundabout way) in recent times. Paul Wiegert of the University of Western Ontario has determined that the dark comet D/1895 Q1 (Swift) interacted with NASA's Mariner 4 Mars probe in 1967. Given that the comet was only ever observed in 1895/1896, there is not enough data to be absolutely certain, but something crossed paths with the probe, and a dark comet is the leading candidate.

Many lost comets could be coming close to Earth in 2012, but without recent observations, there is no way of accurately calculating their passage.

A long period comet would be the best candidate for a 2012 culprit for two reasons:

- an ancient civilization may have tracked comets for much longer than our present civilization, giving them a great advantage in determining the periodicy of long period comets
- a longer period that adds up to a 2012 rendezvous is more statistically reliable than that of a short period comet. Every passage increases the chance of permutations due to encounters with the gravity of planets it may pass. A comet that has orbited 4 times in the last 2000 years is more likely to still be on course than one that has orbited unseen 50 times in the last 200 years.

Summary

Even without the possible return of Comet Caesar, dark comets are the leading contender for triggering a predictable 2012 cataclysm. Comets were known to the ancients - we have many ancient texts providing us with descriptive names like "fire from the sky" - and their cyclical nature makes it easy for any civilization with mathematical prowess to predict. Thousands of hypothetical dark comets remain undiscovered in modern times, and if we do find one on a collision course with our planet, we may only have a few years, or even a few days, to prepare. And those times will be times of mass panic.

Notes

1. Steel, *Rogue Asteroids and Doomsday Comets*, 25. The longest observed orbital period for a comet is 153P/Ikeya-Zhang with 341 years, having been discovered in 1661, and again in 2002.

2. Gribbin, *Fire on Earth*, 103

3. Of course there is the possibility that the Great Comet of 1106AD and the 44BC comet are one and the same. If that were true, it could be expected to return circa 2250AD.

4. Lewis, *Rain of Fire and Ice*, 17

5. Parsons, "'Dark' comets may pose threat to Earth."

6. Ibid.

Addendum

Teleilat Ghassul is located in the Jordan Valley near the Dead Sea is an important site from the Chalcolithic period. Many of the mud brick homes that have been unearthed featured remarkable wall paintings. Paintings were not permanent - it was common for old paintings to be coated with a white lime plaster, and new paintings taking their place. Up to 20 successive layers have been found. Perhaps this 2-metre mural was kept because it represented an important or memorable event:

This is pure speculation, but just as the coin depicted above used an eight-pointed star to represent Comet Caesar, perhaps this is a record of the same comet, but from a different era? For the idea to have any merit, a date for the mural should fit closely the dates I have listed for any previous returns there may have been - 1064BC, 2089BC or 31143BC.

Various radiocarbon dates have been taken from the site, from dung, cereal and wood, and those dates suggest that the occupation lasted roughly 1000 years, ending at approximately 3800BC. The paintings themselves do not seem to have been dated, nor would there be any reason to do so. One must conclude that the most likely date for the painting would be during the period of occupation, so possibly it represents the return of Comet Caesar prior to 3114BC, somewhere around 4139BC.

There are also two comet images at Megiddo, and these have been assigned a date of Early Bronze Age I, which is 3300-3000 BC in the Near East, and fits our 3114BC date perfectly. They were found on paving stones.

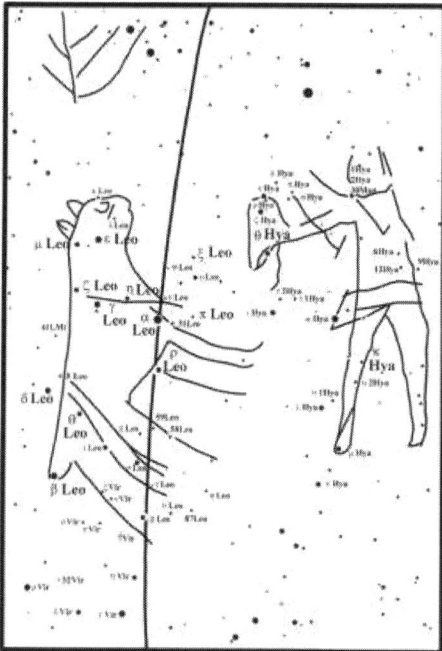

The broom shape is actually a very common way of depicting comets in many ancient cultures, including the Chinese.

INYO   INYO   SAN BERNARDINO

FRESNO   INYO   SIERRA

VENTURA

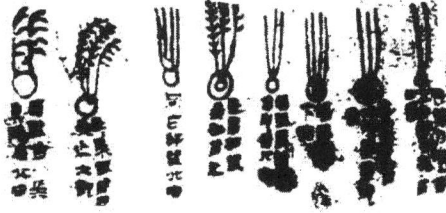

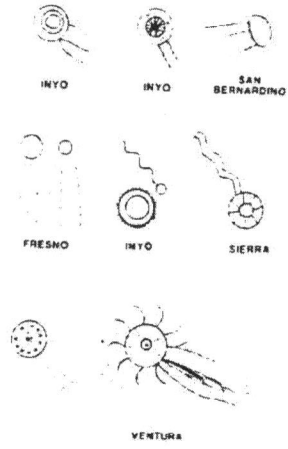

Furthermore, a controversial theory suggests a major asteroid impact dated 3123BC, extremely close to the start of the Long Count calendar.

Appendix 4 – Super Volcanoes

There is nothing to suggest that any ancient civilization would have been able to predict volcanic eruptions thousands of years hence. Therefore the inclusion of this section is due to super-volcanoes fitting the global cataclysm category, and because we shouldn't rule out any possibilities, no matter how remote. Also, keep in mind that a pole shift type event might be predictable, and a pole shift could be the trigger for an eruption - so they don't necessarily happen in their own due course.

In general, if a global cataclysm triggers volcanic eruptions, active volcanoes presently exist on every continent except for Australia. But the type of volcano that can single-handedly harm the entire planet in a substantial manner is a super volcano.

What is a Supervolcano?

A supervolcano is an arbitrary definition for volcanoes that can have the largest of eruptions. It is such a recent term, the spelling of the word is not yet set in concrete, but we'll use the spelling most commonly used. While there is no precise measurement used to qualify a volcano as "super", the word is used to describe a volcano that can threaten global civilization. A supervolcano will either wipe out all of humankind, or make a very good attempt to do so. It is the only local, natural event that has such power, and ranks alongside comets and asteroids as a force of nature we should fear.

Supervolcanoes tend to be active over millions of years. They erupt less frequently than other volcanoes, but when they do erupt, they are substantially more intense. They are rare enough to be missing from modern history, and we only know they have ever occurred due to geological studies of the clues they have left for us.

Supervolcanoes of the Past

These are the largest supereruptions we are aware of - they all have a Volcanic Explosivity Index of 8 (VEI-8) which means they have thrown out at least 1,000 km³ Dense Rock Equivalent of ejecta. The level of ejecta is the most important criteria in terms of risk to the survival of our species. Local disasters will not affect our continued existence, but this level of ash in the atmosphere will create immense difficulties for the entire planet.

26,500 years ago - Lake Taupo, NZ - 1,170 km³
74,000 years ago - Lake Toba, Sumatra - 2,800 km³
254,000 years ago - Whakamaru, NZ - 1,200-2,000 km³
640,000 years ago - Yellowstone, USA - 1,000 km³
2.1 million years ago - Yellowstone, USA - 2,500 km³
2.5 million years ago - Cerro Galan, Argentina - 1,050 km³
4 million years ago - Atana Ignimbrite, Chile - 2,500 km³
4.5 million years ago - Yellowstone, USA - 1,800 km³
6.6 million years ago - Yellowstone, USA - 1,500 km³
27.8 million years ago - La Garita Caldera, USA - 5,000 km³
29.5 million years ago - Sam Ignimbrite, Yemen - 5,550 km³

As an indication of how massive these supereruptions were, Mt St Helens had just 1.2 km³ of ejecta, and Krakatoa had 25km³.

While it might be possible to discern eruption patterns for individual volcanoes, collectively it becomes much more random. Hopefully scientists will be able to forewarn us of the next one to blow.

How Bad Can a Supervolcano Be?

The supereruption of Toba caused temperatures to drop globally by between 3 and 9 degrees Farenheit, as much as 18 degrees in some places, killed 80-90% of humans and destroyed as much as three-quarters of all vegetation in the Northern Hemisphere (1). Substantial amounts of ash were distributed across southern Asia. In India, the ash was typically six inches thick, and at one site it reached an extraordinary depth of twenty feet (2).

Tephra is the fragmental material created by a volcanic eruption. Different types of tephra are determined by size - anything larger than 2.5 centimetres is called a "bomb", and ash is the smallest. Volcanic ash is quite different to the ash you get from burning something. Because it is a fragment of glass or rock, it has sharp edges - if you breathe it in, it will damage your lungs. These tiny pieces will combine with the moisture in your lungs and form a type of cement.

The eruption of Mount Tambora in 1815 was minor compared to a supereruption, but serves as an example of the types of problems we could face. It ejected an estimated 36 cubic miles of ash and pumice, rising as much as 30 miles into the stratosphere. This cloud drifted around the world, visually affecting the atmosphere above both Europe and the USA. Many places suffered their worst winter on record. The winter at Yale University, in Connecticut USA, was 7°F below average. In Europe, food shortages were commonplace. Riots broke out, and armed groups looted farms. Ireland was worst hit, where the famine was believe to cause the spread of typhus, infecting 1.5 million people and killing 65,000. It was known as the *Year Without Summer*. In the last 600 years, only one year has been colder - 1601, following the eruption of a Peruvian volcano.

The famous Krakatoa eruption of 1883 caused a series of tsunamis, up to 100 feet in height, killing tens of thousands of people. The final explosion was defeaning, and was heard 3,000 miles away. Research into some likely large eruptions from 6th century (El Chichon) and 13th century (Proto Krakatoa) suggest that they may have also caused famines, in each case leading to a wipespread plague outbreak, and possibly, in the case of the former, causing the Dark Ages.

Chlorine gases emitted can damage the ozone layer. On top of the damage we have already inflicted via CFCs, the eruption of a supervolcano could deplete the ozone layer to such an extent that it becomes another deadly side-effect. The increase in ultra-violet radiation would cause skin cancer in humans and damage crops.

The excellent *Supervolcano*, by Dr John Savino & Marie D. Jones, includes an in-depth, fictional account of a Long Valley supereruption. Based on current scientific understandings, it is compelling reading. Here's a brief excerpt:

Within days and weeks of the supereruption, the suspension of air routes, the inability to bring cargo in and out of the most deeply affected areas, and the virtual decimation of the Grain Belt, the area of our nation responsible for the vast majority of our grain food sources, all contribute to a growing sense of desperation and panic among survivors anxious to find food. It only takes 0.04 inches of ash to close airports, and the wide swath of blanketed ash would literally shut down every major and minor airport for thousands of miles across the country.

Because even a small amount of ash can clog an engine, road transportation is heavily curtailed, and trucks and machines normally engaged in the moving of supplies from one state to another find themselves immobilized. Electrical equipment shorts out, and wide areas experience power outages and rolling blackouts, rendering communication via computers and phones obsolete.

The description continues, pointing out the importance of short-wave radios. They tell of food riots and contaminated water, of violence and anarchy. Although the USA is the worst hit, the suffering is global. Greatly decreased food production means mass starvation and social unrest. It is a truly horrific scenario. While we can only hope and pray it does not happen in our lifetime, it will certainly happen one day. It would be extremely unlikely that mankind can ever tame even the smallest of volcanoes, so it would appear that a global catastrophe via a supervolcano is entwined in human destiny.

Candidates for a 2012 Eruption

We know of roughly 50 supervolcanoes that have ever existed, and most of those are now extinct. Others are believed to be dormant, while a few are currently active - listed here under their common names:

Toba (Sumatra, Indonesia) - supereruption 74,000 years ago, which was the largest volcanic eruption anywhere on Earth within the last 25 million years. Most humans did not survive this eruption, and in theory it caused a population bottleneck that may have contributed to our evolution, or at least our genetic makeup. Toba may have been active within the last several hundred years.

Yellowstone (USA) - last erupted 630,000 years ago. It has been speculated that the force of a Yellowstone eruption would be the equivalent of one thousand Hiroshima bombs exploding per second (3).

Long Valley (California, USA) - last erupted 760,000 years ago (600 km³ of ejecta).

Valles Caldera (New Mexico, USA) - last erupted 1.15 million years ago (600 km³ of ejecta).

Lake Taupo (New Zealand) - supereruption just 26,500 years ago. Has erupted roughly every thousand years since, with the most recent, 1,800 years ago, being considered the largest in recorded history, 100x larger than Mt St Helens. Fortunately it was NOT recorded, for New Zealand was yet to be settled by humans.

Phlegraean Fields (Naples, Italy) - supererupted 39,000 years ago (500 km³ of ejecta), with other major eruptions since. Could have a major eruption within decades.

Active - but no evidence they are capable of wiping us out:

Kikai Caldera (Japan) - supererupted 6,300 years ago. Still active, with minor eruptions occuring as recently as 2004.

Laacher See (Germany) - potentially still active, erupted 12,900 years ago.

Mount Tambora (Sumbawa, Indonesia) - last erupted in 1815, killing at least 71,000 people.

Aira (Japan) - erupted 22,000 years ago (400 km³ of ejecta), but is still very active. In 1914 an eruption caused the evacuation of 23,000 people. The city of Kagoshima is very close by.

Yellowstone

The Yellowstone caldera is an active place, and there are regular reports that could cause some people to be concerned. Unfortunately, because we have only been monitoring this area for less than a century, it's impossible to tell whether the current activity is relatively normal, or if it is unusual and an indicator that something is up.

A 25 mile section of the caldera rose 5 inches between 1997 and 2003. Prior to this, the whole caldera has risen, fallen, risen, fallen. Between 1923 and 1975 it rose 3-4 feet. Geysers start and stop mysteriously. In an average year the region has thousands of earthquakes too small for people to feel underneath them.

Paranoid folk might want to keep their eye on the Yellowstone Webcam (http://www.nps.gov/archive/yell/oldfaithfulcam.htm)

Long Valley

Long Valley is rated by the U.S. Geological Survey as a bigger risk than Yellowstone. Magma is bubbling beneath the surface, and strong earthquakes are not uncommon - in 1980 it had four which measured 6 on the Richter Scale. Paoha Island in the neaby Mono Lake was created from an eruption just 350 years ago.

Phlegraean Fields

This caldera is also showing signs of unrest. Containing a large portion of the city of Naples, a supereruption similar to the one 39,000 years ago would devestate Europe. Since the late 60s the caldera has risen by 3 metres. Even more worrying, scientists are preparing to drill into the volcano, an act that some experts consider irresponsible, and could result in an eruption.

Recent comparison

In early 2010 the Icelandic volcano Eyjafjallajokull caused weeks of travel chaos, due to airlines not willing to risk their engines by flying jets in zones that could be stricken with ash. In the greater scheme of things this is a minor volcano, yet it still managed to grind local air travel to a halt. A supervolcanic eruption would render us completely useless...

Government to the Rescue?

Two years prior to the Mt St Helens eruption of 1980, scientists predicted that an eruption would occur within 22 years. But would such information be made public about an imminent Yellowstone eruption? For example, if a study predicted an eruption in the next 10 years, the economic upheaval created by half of America relocating could be too much to bear. Leaders might choose to ignore the possibility and cross their fingers. Like they (unfortunately) did with New Orleans. Plenty of conspiracy theorists have discussed the possibility of governmental secrecy (at Above Top Secret forum, the Yellowstone topic has over 600 pages of posts), but of course proof is lacking otherwise it would be fact, not theory.

Where is Safe?

The relative lack of volcanoes make Australia and southern Africa the places to be...

Having said that, Australia may not have any *active* volcanoes, but it did, and it will. The most recent eruptions occured in South Australia (5,000 years ago), Victoria (10,000 years ago) and Queensland (13,000 years ago). For millions of years the level of activity in Australia has been decreasing, but small eruptions are still likely in the future. See *The Volcanic Earth* by Lin Sutherland for details and maps of Australian volcanoes. It also includes future scenarios, and predicts that eruptions that could affect us would be small, with the main hazards being lava flow and bushfires. Australian eruptions would be a minor inconvenience compared to the climatic disturbances for Australia coming from supervolcanic eruptions elsewhere.

Resources

Some useful, official sites, for monitoring Yellowstone:

Yellowstone Webcams
http://www.nps.gov/archive/yell/oldfaithfulcam.htm

Yellowstone Volcano Observatory
http://volcanoes.usgs.gov/yvo/

Frequently asked questions about recent findings at Yellowstone Lake
http://volcanoes.usgs.gov/yvo/new.html

This official site describes actions to take in an ash fall situation :
http://volcanoes.usgs.gov/ash/todo.html

And one non-official site with plenty of info:
http://www.solcomhouse.com/yellowstone.htm

Sources

(1) Supervolcano, by Dr John Savino & Marie D. Jones p37
(2) Supervolcano, by Dr John Savino & Marie D. Jones p123
(3) Supervolcano, by Dr John Savino & Marie D. Jones p37

Additional Resources

Survive2012.com – the author's main site, with many additional articles available

Survive2012.com/news – the author's blog

2012Base.com – a directory of 2012-related websites, hundreds listed

2012Connect.com – a social network just for 2012ers

2012Forum.com – the largest and friendliest 2012 discussion board

2012News.com – news relating to the 2012 meme

2012Wiki.com – the only wiki dedicated to 2012

Thanks to:

- My wife and family for putting up with a writer
- Friends and relations that didn't totally dismiss my odd thoughts
- Patrick Geryl for sharing his ideas over the years
- Members of 2012Forum.com for stimulating conversation
- All the people who I have debated with
- Nature, to be both feared and loved

Life is precious.

2927590R00080

Printed in Great Britain
by Amazon.co.uk, Ltd.,
Marston Gate.